D0902280

CROSSWORDS WORD SEARCHES
LOGIC PUZZLES & SURPRISES!

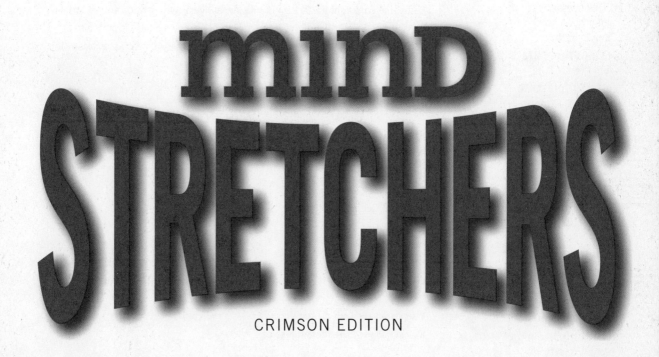

mind STRETCHERS

CRIMSON EDITION

EDITED BY ALLEN D. BRAGDON

Reader's Digest

The Reader's Digest Association, Inc.
New York / Montreal

Project Staff

PROJECT EDITOR
Robert Ronald

PUZZLE EDITOR
Allen D. Bragdon

PRINCIPAL PUZZLE AUTHORS
Peter De Schepper
Frank Coussement
John M. Samson
Sam Bellotto Jr.

CONTRIBUTING PUZZLE AUTHOR
Ron Grosset

SERIES ART DIRECTOR
Andrée Payette

DESIGNER
Hugo Breingan

PRODUCTION ART
Chris A. Cant

ILLUSTRATIONS
BrainSnack®

COPY EDITOR
Judy Yelon

PROOFREADER
Penny Grearson

**MANAGER, ENGLISH BOOK
EDITORIAL**
Pamela Johnson

VICE PRESIDENT, BOOK EDITORIAL
Robert Goyette

The Reader's Digest Association, Inc.

**PRESIDENT AND
CHIEF EXECUTIVE OFFICER**
Robert Guth

**EXECUTIVE VICE PRESIDENT, RDA
& PRESIDENT, NORTH AMERICA**
Dan Lagani

**EXECUTIVE VICE PRESIDENT, RDA
& PRESIDENT, ALLRECIPES.COM**
Lisa Sharples

**EXECUTIVE VICE PRESIDENT, RDA
& PRESIDENT, EUROPE**
Dawn Zier

Individual puzzles are the copyrighted property of the puzzle authors.
BrainSnack® is a registered trademark.

Copyright © 2011 by The Reader's Digest Association, Inc.
Copyright © 2011 by Reader's Digest Association (Canada) ULC
Copyright © 2011 by The Reader's Digest Association Far East Ltd.
Philippine Copyright © 2011 by The Reader's Digest Association Far East Ltd.
All rights reserved. Unauthorized reproduction, in any manner, is prohibited.
Reader's Digest is a registered trademark of The Reader's Digest Association, Inc.

ISBN 978-1-55475-097-9

Address any comments about *Mind Stretchers, Crimson Edition* to:

Reader's Digest Association (Canada) ULC
Book Series Editor
1100 Rene-Levesque Blvd. West
Montreal, Quebec H3B 5H5
Canada

To order copies of this or other editions of the *Mind Stretchers* book series,
call 1-800-846-2100 in the United States and 1-800-465-0780 in Canada.

Visit us on the Web, in the United States at **rd.com**
and in Canada at **readersdigest.ca**

Printed in the United States of America

Contents

Dear Puzzler,

Here I am—figuratively chewing my pencil as I try to concentrate.

The puzzles in this edition of Mind Stretchers demand concentration while challenging a variety of brain skills, including our ability to remember.

Most complaints about memory have nothing to do with the actual ability of the brain to remember things. They come from a failure to focus properly on the task at hand. The brain tunes out inputs that don't spell S-U-R-V-I-V-A-L. Remembering the name of your girlfriend's cat, for example, is probably not the most important thing on your mind, and if you are to succeed you need to stop for a moment and concentrate on linking its name to someone or something that will help you to recall it in the future.

As the brain ages, vocabulary may remain strong in the memory, but the ability to spot meanings and search for the word you are looking for slows down:

Two elderly couples were visiting each other and went out for a walk. The two men, John and Joe, were walking ahead.

"We found a great restaurant last night," said Joe.

"What is it called?" John asked.

They stopped for a moment. Joe scratched his head and then said, "You know, we've been married for over fifty years, but my memory's not so great. Help me out. What is the name of the flower that has a really thorny stem? The red one that is popular on Valentine's Day?"

John replied,, "You mean the rose?"

Joe said, "Yes that's it, of course—the rose!"

He turned back and called out to his wife, "Rose, what was the name of that restaurant we were in last night?"

Language puzzles exercise those circuits that can help lessen forgetful moments and shorten their duration, but memory cannot become learning without concentration, and without regular maintenance, concentration shrinks with age. Puzzles in this edition of Mind Stretchers provide many opportunities for improving and strengthening this important ability and many other useful brain skills:

- pattern and pathfinding puzzles will strengthen your powers of concentration in the same way that physical exercises build aerobic stamina;
- logic and memory puzzles will put a strain on your working memory because you must keep some variables in mind while you test them against others—this frontal-lobe skill is crucial to productive thinking and requires fierce concentration;
- visual and mechanical puzzles will stretch your visual-spatial mental muscles for use in design, architecture, mechanical engineering, exploration and construction;
- divergent thinking puzzles will encourage your ability to think "outside the box" and see links where others see standard differences—an ability that pays off in any profession;
- puzzles involving calculation are important to try—even if you are not a numbers person—for they light up many different parts of the brain at once.

Now, what was that cat called? Large spring?

Ah, that's it—Maxwell!

Allen D. Bragdon

Mind Stretchers Puzzle Editor

■ Meet the Authors

Allen D. Bragdon

Allen describes himself as "the whimsical old dog with puzzle experience and a curious mind." He is a member of the Society for Neuroscience, founding editor of *Games* magazine and editor of the Playspace daily puzzle column, formerly syndicated internationally by *The New York Times*. The author of dozens of books of professional and academic examinations and how-to instructions in practical skills, Allen is also the director of the Brainwaves Center.

PeterFrank

PeterFrank was founded in 2000. It is a partnership between High Performance bvba, owned by Peter De Schepper, and Frank Coussement bvba, owned by Frank Coussement. Together they form a dynamic, full-service content provider specialized in media content.They have more than twenty years of experience in publishing management, art/design and software development for newspapers, consumer magazines, special interest publications and new media.

John M. Samson

John M. Samson is currently editor of Simon & Schuster's *Mega Crossword Series*. His crosswords have appeared on cereal boxes, rock album covers, quilts, jigsaw puzzles, posters, advertisements, newspapers, magazines ... and sides of buildings. John also enjoys painting and writing for the stage and screen.

Sam Bellotto Jr.

Sam Bellotto Jr. has been making puzzles professionally since 1979, when he broke into the business by placing his first sale with *The New York Times Magazine* under then crossword puzzle editor Eugene T. Maleska. Sam has been a regular contributor to Simon & Schuster, *The New York Times*, Random House, and magazines such as *Back Stage*, *Central New York*, *Public Citizen* and *Music Alive!* Bellotto's Rochester, NY-based company, Crossdown, develops word-puzzle computer games and crossword construction software.

When Sam is not puzzling he's out hiking with Petra, his black Labrador dog.

BrainSnack®

The internationally registered trademark BrainSnack® stands for challenging, language-independent, logical puzzles and mind games for kids, young adults and adults. The brand stands for high-quality puzzles. Whether they are made by hand, such as visual puzzles, or generated by a computer, such as sudoku, all puzzles are tested by the target group they are made for before they are made available. In order to guarantee that computer-generated puzzles can actually be solved by humans, BrainSnack® makes programs that only use human logic algorithms.

■ Meet the Puzzles

Mind Stretchers is filled with a delightful mix of classic and new puzzle types. To help you get started, here are instructions, tips and examples for each.

WORD GAMES

Crossword Puzzles

Clues. Clues. Clues.

Clues are the deciding factor that determines crossword-solving difficulty. Many solvers mistakenly think strange and unusual words are what make a puzzle challenging. In reality, crossword constructors generally try to avoid grid esoterica, opting for familiar words and expressions.

For example, here are some actual clues you'll be encountering and their respective difficulty levels:

LEVEL 1   Normandy city
LEVEL 2   Colorado gold rush slogan
LEVEL 3   Miguel hit
LEVEL 4   *Alfred* composer
LEVEL 5   Anglo-Saxon governors

Clues to amuse. Clues to educate. Clues to challenge your mind.

All the clues are there—what's needed now is your answers.

Happy solving!

Word Searches

by PeterFrank

Both kids and grownups love 'em, making word searches one of the most popular types of puzzle. In a word search, the challenge is to find hidden words within a grid of letters. In the typical puzzle, words can be found in vertical columns, horizontal rows or along diagonals, with the letters of the words running either forward or backward. Usually, you'll be given a list of words to find. But to make word searches harder, puzzle writers sometimes just point you in the right direction—they might tell you to find 25 foods, for example. Other twists include allowing words to take right turns, or leaving letters out of the grid.

Hints: *One of the most reliable and efficient searching methods is to scan each row from top to bottom for the first letter of the word. So if you are looking for "violin," you would look for the letter "v." When you find one, look at all the letters that surround it for the second letter of the word (in this case, "i"). Each time you find a correct two-letter combination (in this case, "vi"), you can then scan either for the correct three-letter combination ("vio") or the whole word.*

Word Sudoku

by PeterFrank

Sudoku puzzles have become hugely popular, and our word sudoku puzzles bring the much-loved challenge to word puzzlers.

The basic sudoku puzzle is a 9 x 9 square grid, split into 9 square regions, each containing 9 cells. You need to complete the grid so that each row, each column and each 3 x 3 frame contains the nine letters from the black box above the grid.

There is always a hidden nine-letter word in the diagonal from top left to bottom right.

EXAMPLE	SOLUTION

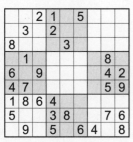

NUMBER GAMES

Sudoku

by PeterFrank

The original sudoku number format is amazingly popular the world over due to its simplicity and challenge.

The basic sudoku puzzle is a 9 x 9 square grid, split into 9 square regions, each containing 9 cells. Complete the grid so that each row, each column and each 3 x 3 frame contains every number from 1 to 9.

As well as classic sudoku puzzles, you'll also find sudoku X puzzles, where the main diagonals must also include every number from 1 to 9, and sudoku twins with two overlapping grids.

Kakuro

by PeterFrank

These puzzles are like crosswords with numbers. There are clues across and down, but the clues are numbers. The solution is a sum which adds up to the clue number.

Each number in a black area is the sum of the numbers that you have to enter in the next empty boxes. The empty boxes that make up the sum are called a run. The sum of the across run is written above the diagonal in the black area, while the sum of the down run is written below the diagonal.

Runs can contain only the numbers 1 through 9, and each number in a run can only be used once. The gray boxes contain only odd numbers and the white contain only even numbers.

LOGIC PUZZLES

Binairo

by PeterFrank

Binairo puzzles look similar to sudoku puzzles. They are just as simple and challenging but that is where the similarity ends.

There are two versions: odd and even. The even puzzles feature a 12 x 12 grid. You need to complete the grid with zeros and ones, until there are 6 zeros and 6 ones in every row and every column. No more than two of the same number can be next to or under each other. Rows or columns with exactly the same combination are not allowed.

EXAMPLE   SOLUTION

The odd puzzles feature an 11 x 11 grid. You need to complete the grid with zeros and ones until there are 5 zeros and 6 ones in every row and column.

Keep Going

In this puzzle, start on a blank square of your choice and connect as many blank squares as possible with one single continuous line.

You can only connect squares along vertical and horizontal lines, not along diagonals. You must continue the connecting line up until the next obstacle—i.e. the rim of the box, a black square or a square that has already been used.

You can change direction at any obstacle you meet. Each square can only be used once. The number of blank squares left unused is marked in the upper square. There is more than one solution, but we only include one solution in our answer key.

EXAMPLE   SOLUTION

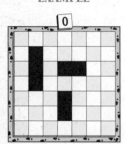
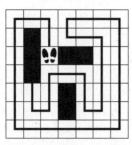

Number Cluster

by PeterFrank

Number Cluster puzzles are language-free, logical numerical problems. They consist of cubes on a 6 x 6 grid. Numbers have been placed in some of the cubes, while the rest are empty. Your challenge is to complete the grid by creating runs of the same number and length as the number supplied. So where a cube with the number 5 has been included on the grid, you need to create a run of five number 5's, including the cube already shown. The run can be horizontal, vertical, or both horizontal and vertical.

EXAMPLE   SOLUTION

Word Pyramid

Each word in the pyramid has the letters of the word above it, plus a new letter.

Start with the answer to No.1 and work your way to the base of the pyramid to complete the word pyramid.

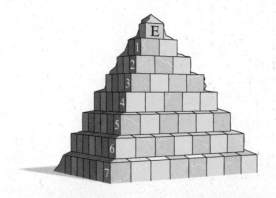

Sport Maze

This puzzle is presented on a 6 x 6 grid. Your starting point is indicated by a red cell with a ball and a number. Your objective is to draw the shortest route from the ball to the goal, the only square without a number. You can only move along vertical and horizontal lines, but not along diagonals. The figure on each square indicates the number of squares the ball must be moved in the same direction. You can change direction at each stop.

EXAMPLE   SOLUTION

Cage the Animals

This puzzle presents you with a zoo divided into a 16 x 16 grid. The different animals on the grid need to be separated. Draw lines that will completely divide up the grid into smaller squares, with exactly one animal per square. The squares should not overlap.

EXAMPLE   SOLUTION

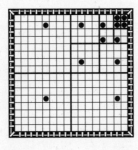

Throughout *Mind Stretchers* you will find unique mazes, visual conundrums and other colorful challenges. Each comes with a new name and unique instructions. Our best advice? Patience and perseverance. Your eyes will need time to unravel the visual secrets.

BrainSnack® Puzzles

To solve a BrainSnack® puzzle, you must think logically. You'll need to use one or several strategies to detect direction, differences and/or similarities, associations, calculations, order, spatial insight, colors, quantities and distances. A BrainSnack® ensures that all the brain's capacities are fully engaged. These are brain sports at their best!

Weather Charts

We all want to know the weather forecast, and here's your chance to figure it out! Arrows are scattered on a grid. Each arrow points toward a space where a weather symbol should be, but the symbols cannot be next to each other vertically, horizontally or diagonally. A symbol cannot be placed on top of an arrow. You must determine where the symbols should be placed.

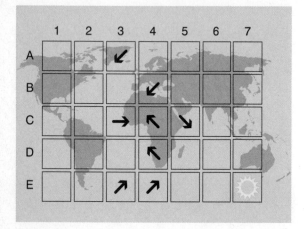

BRAIN TEASERS

You'll also find more than 100 short brain teasers scattered throughout these pages. These puzzles, found at the bottom of the page, will give you a little light relief from the more intense puzzles while still challenging you.

• ONE LETTER LESS OR MORE

• LETTERBLOCKS

• BLOCK ANAGRAM

SHADY OIL *(leisure time away from work)*

☐ ☐ ☐ ☐ ☐ **A** ☐ ☐

• DOODLE PUZZLE

• SQUIRCLES

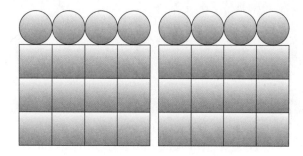

But wait—there's more!

There are additional brain teasers at the top of odd numbered pages, organized into two categories:

• QUICK!: These tests challenge your ability to instantly calculate numbers or recall well-known facts.

• DO YOU KNOW...: These more demanding questions probe the depth of your knowledge of facts and trivia.

■ Master Class:

GET IN THE MOOD TO THINK!

David Gamon is a longtime friend and co-author. He has his doctorate in linguistics and his mind in constant motion. We asked him how he gets in a mood to think hard. We have edited his response to fit the space we have here.

Our culture tends to draw distinctions between "work" and "play" that the brain does not make. The following list is inspired by the insight that it's good for your brain to play—not just as a break from work, but in order to put the brain into the mood to work.

1. GET A DOPAMINE HIGH

Dopamine is a neurotransmitter, a natural chemical released by the brain to carry signals from one electrically charged cell to other cells. As the cells start to work, dopamine changes the person's conscious mood to a calm, alert sense that "all is right with the world."

The dopamine networks evolved to encourage the human brain to engage in these specialized survival functions:

1. to explore new things in terms of past experience;
2. to solve problems in creative ways;
3. to practice and maintain the kinds of cognitive flexibility and mental focus needed for abstract reasoning, logic, and many of the left-brain skills used in scientific thinking.

Dopamine rewards you for doing mental work, especially when the tasks are novel and interesting.

Warm Up Your Dopamine Systems

In the puzzles below, what goes in the blank space to continue the sequence? Each puzzle has a different logic to the pattern you have to figure out to get the answer. As you keep looking for a new strategy, the ongoing novelty helps to keep your dopamine levels high. The puzzles start out easy and then get a little harder, but the harder the problem, the better it feels to solve it.

Blowhard hardhat hatcheck ___mate

Snit in snot on prod or mode __

Gum gun bar bat sun sup lip ____

Bird crane stretch sprint run snag lozenge mint new note ____ beak

7913 992 488 569 72155 614 ___

37210 2 19903 1 48737 3 52209 9
      47391 ___

(The answers are at the end of this master class.)

2. STOP ME IF YOU'VE HEARD THIS ONE ...

Humor is an act of cognitive restructuring which goes well beyond the physical act of laughing. It creates a mental and emotional distance from a potentially stressful situation or problem. It also may change perspective enough to lead to a better solution to the problem. The kind of set-shifting and cognitive flexibility leading up to the emotional sensation of humor also invites creativity. It is a form of mental exercise that's a form of cognitive play. It oils the cogs of cogitation.

Maybe the sensation of humor is part of an acknowledgment that not all contradictions need to be resolved. Here's a favorite example, a joke attributed to the Danish nuclear physicist Niels Bohr in Werner Heisenberg's *Science and Religion*: "One of our neighbors in Tisvilde once fixed a horseshoe over the door to his house. When a common friend asked him, 'But are you really superstitious? Do you honestly believe that this horseshoe will bring you luck?' he replied, 'Of course not; but they say it works even if you don't believe in it.'"

The humor seems to lie in the innocent truth within a logical contradiction—the professed, sober disbelief in the goodluck power of the horseshoe alongside the impulse to hedge bets.

Here's another Bohrism to tickle logical thinking: "Never express yourself more clearly than you can think."

3. GO AROUND IN CIRCLES

"Convergent thinking" is supposed to lead to a single right answer. (IQ tests tend to have questions with a single right answer, whether you agree with it or not.)

To limber up the rigorously logical side of your brain try playing with puzzles like the one below. To get the answer, you have to follow the consequences of each statement, keep them clearly in mind, and keep going until one doesn't lead to a contradiction.

A Logic Puzzle

Here are five statements. All may be true, or only some, or only one, or none at all:

1. Only one of these statements is false.
2. Only two of these statements are false.
3. Only three of these statements are false.
4. Only four of these statements are false.
5. All five of these statements are false.

Which, if any, of the five statements is true? (Answers at the end of this master class.)

4. LISTEN TO ALL OF YOUR BRAINS

There are many brains inside the human cranium, each one with its unique way of processing information. Many of them go about their work inside completely subconscious systems. They are where most "hunches," "gut feelings," "intuitions," and, incidentally, "dreams," come from.

When the conscious mind is working on a conceptually challenging problem, those other parts of the brain may be at work while the thinking mind's back is turned.

To benefit from their insights, admit they are there and learn to listen to their subtle voices.

When he was an undergraduate at MIT, Richard Feynman taught himself to remain consciously aware, in sleep, of the content of his dreams and, in some ways, to control them. It sounds bizarre, but it's not hard to learn. In a lucid dream state, try feeding your dreaming mind whatever puzzles you want to give it. It is likely to come up with an unconventional representation of a solution.

5. WATCH THE STRESS

Creativity thrives better in a "rest and digest" brain state than in a "fight or flight" one. In fact, stomach-churning anxiety and healthy curiosity are so incompatible that it's virtually impossible to feel both at once. Acute stress switches off the brain networks used for complex thought, abstract problem solving and knowledge retrieval.

6. PONDER PARADOXES

The point of pondering a Zen Buddhist koan ("What is the sound of one hand clapping?" is a classic example) is to transcend the limits of the rational mind. Paradoxes invite different ways of looking at things. That's the first step to the kind of original thinking that nudges the mind into entertaining questions other people haven't even thought of.

Here are a few examples:
There's no such thing as nonexistence.

I am not really me.

"No" and "meaning" have no meaning.

7. BE WILLING TO BELIEVE WHAT YOU'VE BEEN TAUGHT MIGHT BE WRONG

When Descartes left his formal studies to devote himself to figuring things out for himself, he eventually decided that there were only two things he knew for sure. The one he's most famous for was that he existed. (The other one was that God existed.) Once he had demolished all the time-honored structures, the building he erected was decidedly different from the one he had demolished.

8. JUST DO THE OPPOSITE

Many interesting insights come from turning problems on their head. Here is an example from linguistics:

The real patterns of mental grammar are to be discovered not in the "correct" things people say but in the errors they inadvertently make. The errors reveal the patterns that are least likely to be of the artificial, prescriptive sort they were taught in school.

Freud had the same kind of insight when he chose to study the human psyche by paying attention to slips of the tongue.
The solution may lie in considering why the hound did not bark.

9. INVITE ACCIDENTS

Don't blunt your curiosity by what it is you started out looking for in a bunch of data. Many scientific discoveries are serendipitous— they arise inadvertently from research that was intended to answer a completely different question. As the saying goes: "Am I really lost, or am I just someplace I've never been before?"

10. DON'T MAKE LISTS BEFORE YOU PLAY

Let your mind roam free to play with your needs. Most people sit down first to make a list of steps to achieve a "goal." It may be a good list leading to the wrong goal.

ANSWERS

Warm Up Your Dopamine Systems

1. check (mate)
2. do
3. lit
4. bill
5. 9
6. 9

A Logic Puzzle

The fourth statement: If it's true, then the other four statements are false—no contradiction

Allen D. Bragdon

★ Pet Cats by Michele Sayer

ACROSS

1. *Lemony Snicket* evil count
5. ___ zirconia
10. Nullify a correction
14. TriBeCa neighbor
15. *Androcles and the Lion* locale
16. Not that
17. John in *Tarantula*
18. "___ Constant Sorrow"
19. Chaplin in *Quantum of Solace*
20. Jim Davis cat
22. One close to the soil
24. Arouses admiration in
25. 1965 march site
26. "... ___ yellow submarine"
27. Tiffani of *White Collar*
30. Aerosol sprays
33. Le Pont-Neuf spans it
34. Dockworker's org.
35. Acuff and Clark
36. Bugle sound
37. Piece of cake
38. Cockney inferno
39. At the ready
40. "1 inch = 10 miles," e.g.
41. Grows steadily
43. Pie ___ mode
44. Live and breathe
45. Churchill Downs sights
49. Samples
51. The Simpsons' first cat
52. Dortmund duck
53. Time after time
55. "Fits you to ___!"
56. Egyptian sun god
57. Bench-clearer
58. Auberjonois of *Deep Space Nine*
59. Shopping place
60. Samurai weapon
61. "Darn!"

DOWN

1. Missouri tributary
2. *South Pacific* director
3. ___ *Day's Night* (1964)
4. Gives up
5. "Action!" preceder
6. Russian peaks
7. Give a little
8. Sea goddess who saved Odysseus
9. Jolt in Jolt
10. Weather radar red areas
11. Mary McDhui's pet cat
12. ___ *kleine Nachtmusik*
13. Imperialist of yore
21. McKellen and McEwan
23. Not aweather
25. Tank top
27. Eye drops
28. Mideast carrier
29. A barber may shave this
30. Talking horse
31. Captive of Hercules
32. Granny's pet cat
33. "George Washington ___ Here"
36. Flowers
37. Sword sheath
39. "You can't pray ___"
40. Shredded dish
42. Breadth
43. Answered (for)
45. "That'll teach you!" look
46. Subsequently
47. Kagan of the Supreme Court
48. Icy precip
49. Uniformed unit
50. Pilaster
51. Battle of Normandy site
54. A handful of

★★ Number Cluster

Complete the grid by constituting adjoining clusters that consist of as many cubes as the number on the cubes. At cube 5, for instance, you will have to make a five-cube cluster. Two or more figure cubes of the same value belong to the same cluster. You can only place your cubes along horizontal and/or vertical lines.

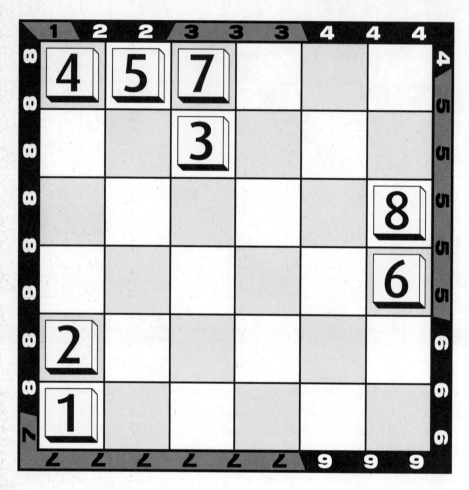

ONE LETTER LESS OR MORE

The word on the right side contains the letters of the word on the left side plus or minus the letter in the middle. One letter is already in the right place.

HAIRLINE -I N ☐ ☐ ☐ ☐ ☐

★ BrainSnack®—Touchdown

Which digit should replace the question mark in the score?

UNCANNY TURN

Rearrange the letters of the phrase to form a cognate anagram, one which is related or connected in meaning to the original phrase. The answer can be one or more words.

ONE LIVE WITNESS

★ Pet Dogs by Michele Sayer

ACROSS

1 Bones of Sleepy Hollow
5 *My Fair Lady* horse race
10 Catch sight of
14 Sitarist Shankar
15 Joe in *Apollo 13*
16 "Elite Eight" org.
17 Where Adam met Eve
18 Something to stake
19 ___ de France
20 Doc Brown's dog
22 "Over the Rainbow" composer Arlen
24 Remote
25 He spied on Joshua
26 Henrietta, NY campus
27 Transported
30 "Ship of the desert"
33 *Baywatch Hawaii* actress Eleniak
34 Dr. of rap
35 "I've Got ___ in Kalamazoo"
36 Airs
37 Arable soil
38 Capek robot play
39 Ebb and others
40 *Memoirs of a Geisha* setting
41 Didn't go
43 "Age cannot wither ___ ..."
44 *Damn Yankees* composer
45 Twelfth graders
49 "Jacob's ___": Huey Lewis
51 Doc's dog on *Fraggle Rock*
52 12th Hebrew month
53 Wake-up call
55 "___ Rock": Simon & Garfunkel
56 Sneaker brand
57 "Walk ___ Man": 4 Seasons
58 Shadowbox
59 Pippin
60 "Card Players Quarreling" artist
61 Frost hair

DOWN

1 AKC category
2 Diameter halves
3 *Mystic Pizza* props
4 Jongleur
5 Gradient
6 Bowling "lily"
7 Scott of *Hawaii Five-0*
8 "Don't Blame It ___" (Congos reggae tune)
9 Woody's voice in *Toy Story*
10 Access
11 Shaggy's Great Dane
12 Giamatti in *John Adams*
13 Summer sale site
21 Kite stabilizer
23 Thomas ___ Edison
25 Loonies, e.g.
27 Apollo in *Rocky 2*
28 He was, in Latin 101
29 Floor model
30 Ex-NBA player "Big Dog"
31 A fit of shivering
32 Winslow family's Great Dane
33 Where to get down from
36 Necessary nutrients
37 Johnny Mercer, for one
39 10-point Q, e.g.
40 Casino game
42 All mixed up
43 One of the Munsters
45 "Shop 'til you drop" trip
46 1900 zoological discovery
47 Hire a new crew
48 Square one
49 Shoot a film
50 "And every third word ___ ...": Shak.
51 Rice wine
54 Aflame

★ U.S.A.

All the words are hidden vertically, horizontally or diagonally—in both directions. The letters that remain unused form a sentence from left to right.

```
O K L A H O M A M O N T A N A
T H E N L A W I S C O N S I N
V A M E A A M E C R G O A I C
I A L K D I B O S G E M R P N
R R M A R Y L A N D R R I O E
G B V N S O A I M A O E Z B W
I E L S R K M N D A Y V O A J
N R D A E O A I N D I A N A E
I H D S Y G R S R O I A A V R
A O E W I O I D C F I R O M S
A D M H L O E I R S I G A E E
O E C F N G X V I E S P R U Y
C I C I I E E U A M E A K H R
M S L C M H O O A N W T A A N
A L D W S L A I R A L W N O R
I A E W H O W A L G A S S B O
N N K R O Y W E N I I R A N I
E D N F L O D R I E N A S C E
```

LOUISIANA
MAINE
MARYLAND
MICHIGAN
MONTANA
NEVADA
NEW JERSEY
NEW MEXICO
NEW YORK
OKLAHOMA
OREGON
RHODE ISLAND
VERMONT
VIRGINIA
WISCONSIN
WYOMING

ALABAMA
ALASKA
ARIZONA
ARKANSAS

COLORADO
DELAWARE
FLORIDA
GEORGIA

HAWAII
ILLINOIS
INDIANA
KANSAS

CHANGE ONE

Change one letter in each of these two words to form a common two-word phrase.

TWITCH IN

★★ Keep Going

Start on a blank square of your choice and connect as many blank squares as possible with one single continuous line. You can only connect squares along vertical and horizontal lines, not along diagonal lines. You must continue the connecting line up until the next obstacle, i.e. the rim of the box, a black square or a square that has already been used. You can change direction at any obstacle you meet. Each square can only be used once. The number of blank squares that will be left unused is marked in the upper square. There is more than one solution. We only show one solution.

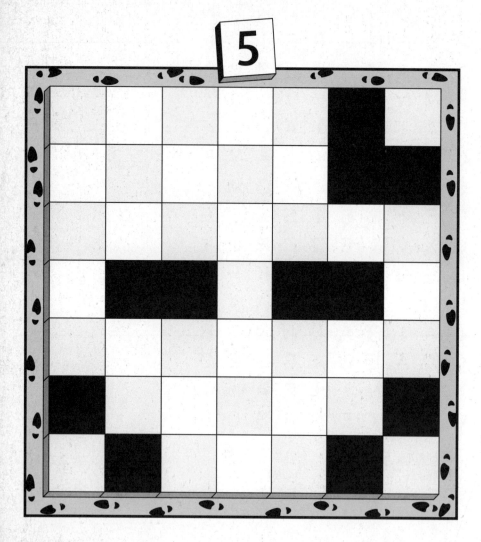

FRIENDS

What do the following words have in common?

ANGEL BISHOP DEACON DUCHESS DUKE ENEMY WAY

★ 2011 Movies I by Cindy Wheeler

ACROSS

1 It's often rolling in the aisles
5 "Scat!"
10 Implored
14 Ancient lyre
15 ___ donna
16 Derby winner ___ Ridge
17 "Later dude!"
18 Last but not ___
19 Jannings in *Quo Vadis*
20 2011 Owen Wilson movie
22 Hands down
24 Ad infinitum
25 "T-R-O-U-B-L-E" singer Travis
26 Suffix for sheep
27 Venetian vessels
30 *Carmen* composer
33 Forearm bones
34 Southern Nigerian
35 Hooplas
36 Thrash about
37 Edvard Munch Museum site
38 *The Aviator* star, to fans
39 ___ *Evil* (Mia Farrow film)
40 Black-ink entry
41 Stop between Tampa and Orlando
43 Sounds of relief
44 Tennis legend Chris
45 Prepped for a race
49 Coats with crumbs
51 2011 Vin Diesel movie
52 *Beverly Hills Cop* org.
53 Midwest hub
55 Gossip column pair
56 Arch with a point
57 Brunch fruit
58 Cubesmith Rubik
59 Troubadour
60 Cheer up
61 Ellipsis trio

DOWN

1 Hoard away
2 From the Far East
3 Creator of Willy (Wonka)
4 Streetcars
5 Make waves
6 Salad plant
7 Firths
8 Weather org.
9 Motherly
10 Copperfield's cry
11 Unbounded
12 Mean business
13 Tim of *Private Practice*
21 Fumigator's target
23 Helper
25 *I Pagliacci* clown
27 Spleen, for one
28 Au fait

29 It's found in a stack
30 Musket ammo
31 Light bulb, figuratively
32 2011 Kevin James film
33 Suffix for fraud
36 Horrific
37 Turned to bone
39 Vehicle with no wheels
40 At the drop of ___ (quickly)
42 Ducked
43 Leblanc's Lupin
45 The Hanged Man, e.g.
46 Safecracker's "soup"
47 Decathlon component
48 Studio tapes
49 Amorphous lump
50 Shankar piece

51 FDR's Scottie
54 Norse death goddess

★★★ Sudoku

Fill in the grid so that each row, each column and each 3 x 3 frame contains every number from 1 to 9.

			6					
4		2			7			
	7	8	2					
7	8	4					2	
2		6	1				3	5
	5	3						
8	4		7	3	5			
				9			7	4
3				6	2	8		9

DOODLE PUZZLE

A doodle puzzle is a combination of images, letters and/or numbers that represent a word or a concept. If you cannot solve a doodle puzzle, do not look at the answer right away. Think hard—and outside the box.

★★★ Sport Maze

Draw the shortest way from the ball to the goal. You can only move along vertical and horizontal lines, not along diagonal lines. The figure on each square indicates the number of squares the ball must be moved in the same direction. You can change direction at each stop.

	5	4	3	5	2
3	4	3	3	2	5
1	2	2	3	4	4
1	1	2	1	4	3
2	1	4	1	3	1
3	5	5	3	1	1

ONE LETTER LESS OR MORE

The word on the right side contains the letters of the word on the left side plus or minus the letter in the middle. One letter is already in the right place.

B A C H E L O R -B ☐ ☐ ☐ L ☐ ☐ ☐

★ 2011 Movies II by Cindy Wheeler

ACROSS

1 Hera's bellicose son
5 Full of oneself
9 German iron center
14 *The Lion King* lioness
15 Sharon in *Valley of the Dolls*
16 Household task
17 2011 Mel Gibson movie
19 W.C. Fields persona
20 Social companions
21 Developed, as a player
23 You, in Paris
24 Post-shower powder
25 Sauce with a kick
29 Malfeasance
32 O'Hara's ___ *to Live*
33 With tongue in cheek
35 Mongrel
36 Sourdough's windfall
37 Armed robbery
38 Common rail
39 NYC time
40 Midler in *Hocus Pocus*
41 *The Seventh Seal* star Max von ___
42 Shilly-shallies
44 Keep bottled up
46 Plot to develop, perhaps
47 Stephen in *The Crying Game*
48 Albums
51 Mime Marcel
55 Earthy pigment
56 2011 Hank Azaria movie
58 Fish basket
59 Fill a ship
60 Mr. Ed's dad
61 Nomads of SE Turkey
62 Olfactory offense
63 Book of Mormon book

DOWN

1 Pot chip
2 Sideline sounds
3 Part of GE: Abbr.
4 Subversion stratagem
5 Not moving
6 Dallas hoopsters, for short
7 Comanche enemy, once
8 Bacterium
9 Extreme joy
10 "Auld Lang Syne" starter
11 2011 Jake Gyllenhaal movie
12 Emerald Isle language
13 "___ You Now": Lady Antebellum
18 Weatherworn
22 Not true
25 *The Canterbury ___*
26 "Kiss From ___": Seal
27 2011 Cameron Diaz movie
28 *Golden Boy* dramatist
29 Man of rare gifts?
30 Currency for Catalonia
31 Box-office boosters
34 Tigers of Henrietta, NY
37 Used a scythe
38 Alma mater of Bob Costas
40 Oil drums
41 Whale species
43 Put one in the net
45 Chalkboard item
48 Stone Age weapon
49 Oatmeal color
50 Normandy city
51 "Love ___": Beatles
52 Leprechaun's land
53 ___-American
54 Applications
57 Once owned

★ Word Sudoku

Complete the grid so that each row, each column and each 3 x 3 frame contains the nine letters from the black box below. The hidden nine-letter-word is in the diagonal from top left to bottom right.

		A	E	G	I	M	S	T	U	Z		

	G						Z
M		Z				I	
					M		E
E					U		
				S		T	
M		S	U	A			
G		U	E	I	T		
Z					U	E	G
A	E			T	I	M	

SANDWICH

What five-letter word belongs between the word at left and the word at right, so that the first and second word, and the second and third word, each form a common compound word or phrase?

OVER _ _ _ _ _ OVER

★★ BrainSnack®—Crazy Cube

Which block (1–9) needs to be removed so that you can combine the three large parts into a single cube?

LETTERBLOCKS

Move the letterblocks around so that words are formed on top and below that you can associate with chess.

A R B T E T Y
P N O N I E G

★ Best of Bob by John M. Samson

ACROSS

1 Chicago paper, casually
5 Alpine pinnacle
10 USSR, in the USSR
14 Hydrogen-fueled forklift
15 Fabric
16 Jai ___
17 Battery for laser pointers
18 Muslim maid of paradise
19 Greatest
20 1969 Bob Dylan song
23 Havens
24 Michael of *Star Trek: TNG*
25 Diane in *Secretariat*
27 Cell division process
30 *Rubyfruit Jungle* author Mae Brown
33 Slightest
35 Cinco minus cuatro
36 1963 Bob Dylan song
40 Suffix for capital
41 Banquet
42 "___ girl!"
43 Ocean floors
45 Perfect place
48 Smell of smoke
49 Puts up a tower
53 1975 Bob Dylan song
58 Yours, in Paris
59 Pastel color
60 *Je Vous* ___ (Deneuve film)
61 Bonn neighbor
62 Temporary contract
63 Mounties, briefly
64 Terminates
65 Asian tents
66 "The ___ the limit!"

DOWN

1 Anatole France novel
2 Gaucho's rope
3 Corporate raider Carl
4 Almond-flavored pastry
5 Home-delivery food company
6 *The Time Machine* slaves
7 Big loss
8 Gillette razor
9 Immature
10 Mustang's 1967 rival
11 Bozo's outfit
12 Señora's home
13 Bleed for
21 Greek vowel
22 Lenya in *The Appointment*
26 Nobelist writer Canetti
27 Picture finish
28 B&B cousins
29 Teetotaler's order
30 Babe Ruth's 2,211
31 Dutch singer DeLange
32 Roseanne's ex
34 Some dashes
37 Bernstein's "___ Pretty"
38 1970 Mick Jagger title role
39 Sommelier settings
44 Commences
46 Clears for liftoff
47 East ender
50 Camera sound
51 Breadbasket
52 Barely flows
53 *I'll ___ You There*: (Oates novel)
54 Like ___ of bricks
55 Joan of Arc's god
56 Ending for cell
57 *Back to the Future* destination

★ Binairo

Complete the grid with zeros and ones until there are 6 zeros and 6 ones in every row and every column. No more than two of the same number can be next to or under each other. Rows or columns with exactly the same content are not allowed. There is only one valid solution.

					1		1				
						1		1		1	
0	1		1		1					1	
								0			
		0		0	0			0			
		0			1					1	
						0					
	0										
		0	0			1	1		1		
							1				0
1					1			0			0
	1		1	0	0		1				

REPOSITION PREPOSITION

Unscramble I DID NOTATION and find a three-word preposition.

★ Spot the Differences

Find the nine differences in the image on the right.

DOUBLETALK

What word means "a doorway" or "delight"?

★ Themeless by Don Law

ACROSS

1 Injured
5 Hide the loot
10 "Got it!"
14 Nonesuch
15 Horse for Tonto
16 "Why don't we!"
17 Like black olives
18 Advantage
19 *Tomb Raider* girl
20 Deviated
22 Harvest goddess
24 Congo fly
25 Like corkwood
26 Saint Catherine's city
28 Plead with
30 "Abdulla Bulbul ___"
32 Chipped beef on ___
34 Greek letter
35 Part of YMCA
36 Kind of reunion
37 Pete's Wicked drinks
38 *Addams Family* cousin
39 Army uniform material
40 Sleep soundly?
41 Field combines
43 Mulligrubs
45 Eared fur seal
46 Disc-golf target
49 ___ Columbia
51 Bijouterie
52 Split
53 Sports artist Neiman
55 Sitar wood
56 Egyptian sun god
57 Wear away
58 *Little Man* ___ (1991)
59 "___ la vie!"
60 Like Cujo
61 Winged deity

DOWN

1 Buchholz in *The Magnificent Seven*
2 College credits
3 House members
4 Covenants
5 Petulance
6 Heading for overtime
7 Film director ___ Lee
8 Dickey button
9 Beyond repair
10 Accuse tentatively
11 *Spin City* star
12 *M*A*S*H* prop
13 Gravelly ridges
21 1914 Belgian battle line
23 Heavy fog
27 Burdened Titan
28 "Go to" language
29 Stocking
30 *The Kite Runner* boy
31 It came from outer space
33 Barrel wood
36 Jeep parent
37 Licorice liqueur
39 Russell in *August Rush*
40 Haddock side
42 Intellectual property
44 Followed orders
47 Sister of Terpsichore
48 Moppets
49 Bric-a-___
50 Olympic queen
51 Long in *All-American Girl*
54 Take inventory?

★ Cage the Animals

Draw lines to completely divide up the grid into small squares with exactly one animal per square. The squares should not overlap.

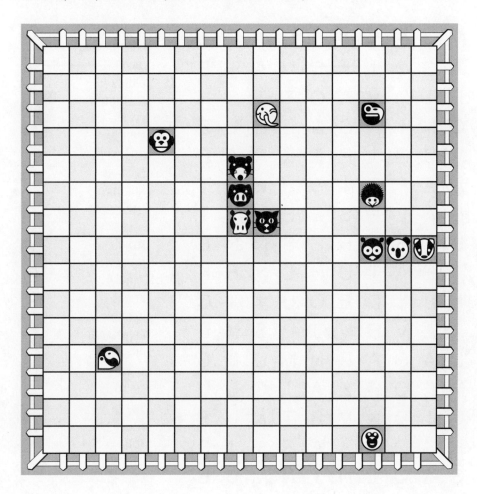

TRANSADDITION

Add one letter to PERMEATING LIVING ROOM and rearrange the rest to find a connection.

★ Jazz

All the words are hidden vertically, horizontally or diagonally—in both directions. The letters that remain unused form a sentence from left to right.

```
J A D Z Z M U S N I D C O R I
A C I R F A G O I A P N A T E
N O I S U F T D V A O T T C H
S N A V E G N I W S B E B L E
E G I N N V S N I R E K R A P
U N G I O A A F T I B H E R T
L O L O S B W L P S E E N I T
B L I M E U T S S H E S C N E
E A O N T T E A T U R L Y E K
A N K M O L B Y D E O U I T C
K N G E L A A V R V J P S M E
S T D I R D A O A R N M U N B
R A G T I M E O H E A I G C U
E O N L R C I D N V B T N H R
E O O S T R S O I A A S I I B
C H O R D S A O E N I N M U E
R H Y T H M B T R U M P E T G
W O R B I G B A N D L E A N S
```

CLARINET
CONTRABASS
DAVIS
DRUGS
ELLINGTON
EVANS
FUSION
GILLESPIE
GUITAR
HOLIDAY
IMPULSE
MILES
MINGUS
MONK
PARKER
PIANO
RAGTIME
REINHARDT
RHYTHM
SLAVES
SOLO
SWING
TRUMPET
TUBA
VERVE
VOODOO

AFRICA
BAKER
BANJO

BASIE
BEBOP
BIG BAND

BLUES
BRUBECK
CHORDS

MISSING LETTER PROVERB

Fill in each missing letter, indicated by an X, to make a well-known proverb.

CLXAXLIXEXS IX NXXX XO XOXLIXEXS

★★ Sunny Weather

Where will the sun shine knowing that each arrow points in the direction of a spot where the symbol is located? The symbols cannot be next to each other vertically, horizontally or diagonally. A symbol cannot be placed on top of an arrow. We show one symbol.

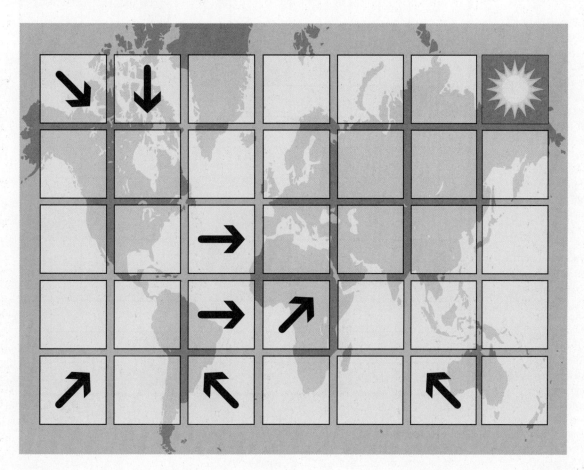

BLOCK ANAGRAM

Form the words that are described in the brackets with the letters above the grid. Extra letters are already in the right place.

RINGBIRD (board on collapsible supports)

| | | O | | N | | | O | A | | |

★ Sleuths by John McCarthy

ACROSS

1 Anglo-Saxon bard
5 #
10 Cabbage salad
14 *Deus* ___ (1976 sci-fi novel)
15 Exactly opposite
16 Mother of Pollux
17 Agatha Christie sleuth
19 Kline in *The Squid and the Whale*
20 Defeats
21 Like five-star hotels
23 Net-worth factor
24 Jewish month
25 Smell awful
27 Lettering aid
30 Printer cartridge
33 Age
35 Tiller's tool
36 Parodied
37 "___ Johnny!"
38 FedExed
39 Southern Iran city
40 Hawkeye Stater
41 U.S. Open winner Safin
42 "Heh-heh," for one
44 Use a rotary phone
46 "Able ___ ere ..."
47 Assistant for Hillary
51 Alligator pear
54 Scintillates
55 "The Persistence of Memory" painter
56 Fictional TV sleuth
58 "A" in code
59 Ache
60 *Breathing Lessons* author Tyler
61 Command to Rover
62 All filled up
63 Knead homophone

DOWN

1 Disney lion
2 Has a bawl
3 Brewery kilns
4 Annoyed
5 Exiguous
6 ___ d'oeuvres
7 Grossglockner, e.g.
8 Chest rattle
9 Bishops and monsignors
10 Catchphrase
11 Ross Macdonald sleuth
12 Yemen capital
13 Kind of ad
18 Length unit
22 First place
26 Mardi Gras group
27 Shell out
28 Macbeth's burial isle
29 Riga resident
30 Barbershop powder
31 Aquarium beauty
32 Rex Stout sleuth
34 *Star Trek* producer Behr
37 Special times
38 Willy Loman, for one
40 "___ most unusual day ..."
41 Hunter of the PGA
43 Kind of profiling
45 *Cast Away* setting
48 Geneva river
49 Al dente order
50 Questioned
51 Esau's wife
52 Batman's friend Vicki
53 Ancient Greek concert halls
54 Prometheus stole it
57 Informant

★ Kakuro

Each number in a black area is the sum of the numbers that you have to enter in the next empty boxes. The empty boxes that make up the sum are called a run. The sum of the across run is written above the diagonal in the black area and the sum of the down run is written below the diagonal. Runs can only contain the numbers 1 through 9 and each number in a run can only be used once. The gray boxes only contain odd numbers and the white only even numbers.

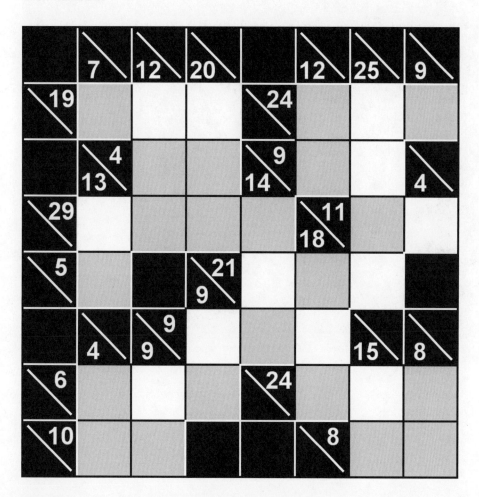

ONE LETTER LESS OR MORE

The word on the right side contains the letters of the word on the left side plus or minus the letter in the middle. One letter is already in the right place.

| I | N | C | R | E | A | S | E | -A | | | C | | | |

★★★ BrainSnack®—Pedal Power

Here are three pairs of cycling gloves. Which glove (1-6) does not belong?

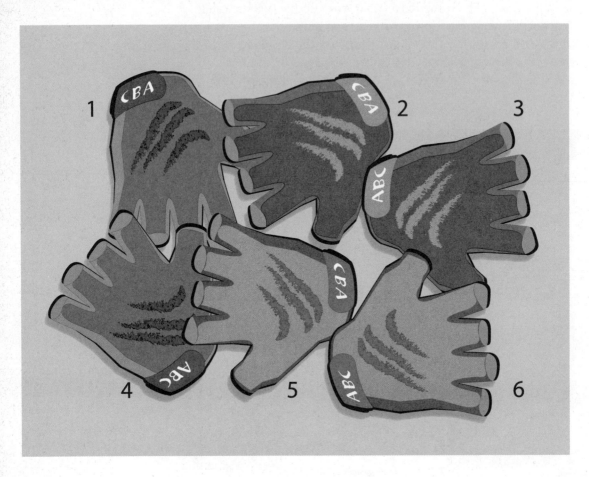

END GAME

The words you are seeking all have the letters END in them in the position indicated.
When you have found all of the answers, from the clues on the right, one column will reveal the
END GAME word but no need to go into it.

							Clue
_	_	_	_	_	E N D		Share of profits
E N D	_	_	_	_			Finishing line
_	_	E N D	_	_	_		Mixing
_	E N D	_	_	_	_		Gently

★ College Teams by Tim Wagner

ACROSS

1 Astrologer's scales
6 "You don't know the ___ of it!"
10 Maple seeds
14 TNT's *Rizzoli & ___*
15 Love, Spanish-style
16 Terrarium plant
17 *Green Eggs and Ham* author
18 South Carolina team
20 Came before
22 Gary in *Apollo 13*
23 Roberto of boxing
24 Rug type
25 White-sale items
27 Overshoes
31 2011 NBA champs
32 Stalwart
34 One may lose this on *Jeopardy!*
35 Owen's *Royal Tenenbaums* role
36 *Alias* org.
37 "Messenger" compound
38 ___ *Well That Ends Well*
40 Artificial movie background
42 Stagehand
43 TV's *The Young and the ___*
45 One thing after another
47 Aggravate
48 Hyperactive
49 Ready for the World hit (with "Oh")
52 Emotionally moving
55 Louisville team
57 *The Nanny Diaries* nanny
58 Shepard's ___ *of the Mind*
59 *Dies* ___ (funeral hymn)
60 Davis in *Beetlejuice*
61 Mrs. Dick Tracy
62 Mudpuppies
63 Car introduced in 1957

DOWN

1 "She sells seashells" problem
2 Czech river
3 Duke team
4 Heroic deeds
5 Affirm
6 Siegfried's murderer
7 Perry's *Diary of ___ Black Woman*
8 *Pink Panther* actor Herbert
9 Anew
10 In the middle of
11 Activity centers
12 Says "Who?"
13 ___ *Quam Videri* (NC motto)
19 "Arrivederci"
21 *The Incredibles* son
24 Nasser's successor
25 Apply haphazardly
26 *Catwoman* actress Berry
27 Alternative to hash browns
28 Miami team
29 Keebler's head elf
30 Hits the roof
33 "As ___ in point ..."
39 Advances
40 Tennis player Oudin
41 *Caprica* actor Morales
42 Imitated the Cheshire Cat
44 Taylor in *The Haunting*
46 Embark on
48 Pentateuch author
49 "Amscray!"
50 In fine fettle
51 Trojan War instigator
52 City map
53 2009 Daniel Day-Lewis film
54 Greenish blue
56 "Bow wow!"

★★ Keep Going

Start on a blank square of your choice and connect as many blank squares as possible with one single continuous line. You can only connect squares along vertical and horizontal lines, not along diagonal lines. You must continue the connecting line up until the next obstacle, i.e. the rim of the box, a black square or a square that has already been used. You can change direction at any obstacle you meet. Each square can only be used once. The number of blank squares that will be left unused is marked in the upper square. There is more than one solution. We only show one solution.

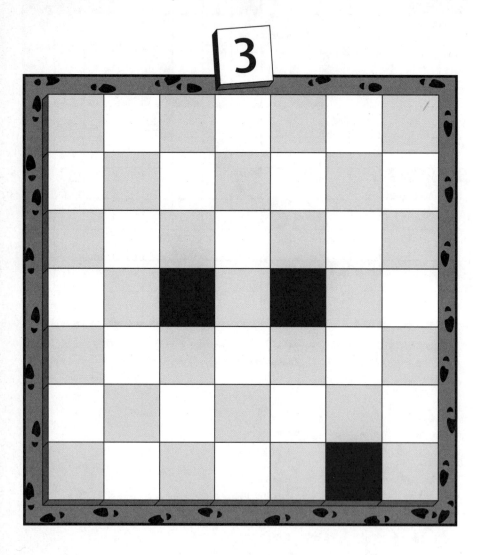

DELETE ONE

Delete one letter from ORATORS HATE and rearrange the rest to find a speaker's fear.

★★★ Sudoku

Fill in the grid so that each row, each column and each 3 x 3 frame contains every number from 1 to 9.

	4						5	9
8			4					
		1		6	9			4
					7			8
2		3						
	4		8	1	6	9	7	
7	8			3	9		4	1
9		1	2	4	7			3

CHANGELINGS

Each of the three lines of letters below spell words which have a nautical connection, but the letters have been mixed up. Four letters from the first word are now in the third line, four letters from the third word are in the second line and four letters from the second word are in the first line. The remaining letters are in their original places. What are the words?

C I A H T H A D S E
H O P S T G U E R K
S L I G W R O C U S

★ Play Ball! by Don Law

ACROSS

1 Annie Oakley's arm
6 Minnow, often
10 Greek house
14 The Ram
15 South African fox
16 Fit or Insight, e.g.
17 18th-century French radical
18 Where Cal Ripken played
20 Affected lover of beauty
22 Blotch
23 "Here, ___ and Everywhere": Beatles
24 Filled with awe
25 Redford in *The Natural*
27 *Damn Yankees* heavy
28 Infante of baseball
29 Acclimatize
31 Snub
35 Pan-American Union successor
36 French donkey
37 Suffix for verb
38 Leg bender
40 Hugh Laurie series
42 "I completely agree!"
43 "Forever" USPS issue
45 Acute
47 "Father of Radio"
50 Band on a barber's chair
51 Agreed with
52 Texas Panhandle city
55 Where Graig Nettles played
57 *Jizzrim 4* novelist
58 Budget item
59 Nutmeg skin
60 Colorful fish
61 Horatian poems
62 Fellow
63 "I thought we had ___!"

DOWN

1 Father Wolf in *The Jungle Book*
2 *Dies* ___ (funeral hymn)
3 Where Stan Musial played
4 Cowhide
5 *Good Times* actress Rolle
6 Moisten with marinade
7 Richmond tennis great
8 Prefix for bar
9 Wood eater
10 Buckles up
11 In need of paving
12 Cornmeal dish
13 Drank like a fish
19 Colosseum wear
21 "Rendezvous" artist
24 Denudes
25 Bamboozle
26 Arab League member
27 Bedtime for a vampire
30 *King Kong* actress Watts
32 What Yogi Berra guarded
33 Web surfer
34 Hawaiian honker
39 Accompanies
40 Etienne Aigner product
41 ___ noche (tonight)
42 Bypassed
44 ___ the line (obeyed)
46 Correction list
47 Montreal subway
48 Called for liniment
49 Bonn river
50 Small food fish
52 Z ___ zebra
53 Pre-euro Italian coin
54 Vocal
56 "You ___ My Sunshine"

★★★ Sport Maze

Draw the shortest way from the ball to the goal. You can only move along vertical and horizontal lines, not along diagonal lines. The figure on each square indicates the number of squares the ball must be moved in the same direction. You can change direction at each stop.

2	1	4	4	2	3
2	3	3	2	2	1
1	2	1	2	2	2
5	4	3	3	4	5
2	4	4	2	1	5
	1	1	4	1	3

LETTER LINE

Put a letter in each of the squares below to make a word which means "to present or announce." These numbered clues refer to other words which can be made from the whole.

4 9 6 7 8 3 1 5 2 MONEY OFF; 1 2 6 7 8 9 PERSUADE;
8 5 2 6 7 1 3 PASSAGE; 4 7 1 2 9 6 DESTROYED.

1	2	3	4	5	6	7	8	9

★ Word Sudoku

Complete the grid so that each row, each column and each 3 x 3 frame contains the nine letters from the black box below. The hidden nine-letter word is in the diagonal from top left to bottom right.

A C D E K O P R S

A	K							
	R				K	E		
	S			A		D		
D		E		C				O
R			K		E			S
O	C		P			A		D
E	R	P	A	D		S	C	K
		C		S				

ONE LETTER LESS OR MORE

The word on the right side contains the letters of the word on the left side plus or minus the letter in the middle. One letter is already in the right place.

M A G A Z I N E -E- □ □ □ **Z** □ □ □

★★★ BrainSnack®—Shirt Number

Every shirt number is calculated based on the three circles. Just like for Roman numerals, a smaller value that precedes a larger value is deducted. Which shirt number should replace the question mark?

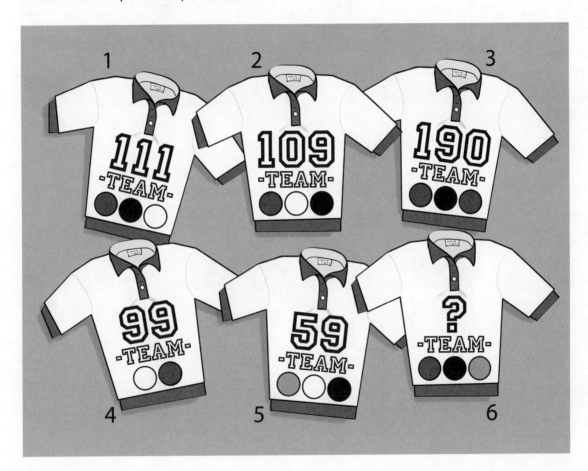

UNCANNY TURN

Rearrange the letters of the phrase to form a cognate anagram, one which is related or connected in meaning to the original phrase. The answer can be one or more words.

CLEAR SPICE PIE

★ Potpourri by Peggy O'Shea

ACROSS

1 Jay or Bill of golf
5 Agreements
10 Excitements
14 Slugs
15 *Goldfinger* prop
16 Reclaimed merchandise
17 Julia in *The Rookie*
18 Backgammon piece
19 "Me too" sort
20 Clambake competition
23 1,101 in Roman numerals
24 A fruit to poach
25 Virginia city
29 Make a patty
32 Son of, in Arabia
33 Razed
35 "Cry ___ River"
36 Tennis replay
37 Schedule letters
38 " ___ tu": Verdi aria
39 Yalie
40 Seventh-inning act
44 Long in *The Best Man*
45 Bend out of shape
47 Raised a glass to
49 Jabba the Hutt's dancer
50 Wee drink
51 Handyman
59 Et ___ (and others)
60 Aerosol propellant
61 Meter money
62 A puck in a net
63 Ditsy
64 Birthplace of Ceres
65 Liquidate
66 Apple gadget
67 Low-pitched

DOWN

1 *Nine to Five* boss
2 *The Joy Luck Club* nanny
3 Chinese border river
4 Long-faced
5 Not care for
6 Cologne duck
7 Enthralled
8 Lengthy
9 Belfry topper
10 Where Noah landed
11 Kind of store
12 "Black gold" bloc
13 Smarting
21 Bionomics: Abbr.
22 Departed
25 Irked
26 Division signs
27 Misanthropic
28 "Ice Maiden" of tennis
29 Lester of bluegrass
30 Spine-tingling
31 Aquatic nymph
34 Summer in Sèvres
40 Go it alone
41 2000 Michael Douglas film
42 *Field of Dreams* star Kevin
43 "Donna" musical
46 *Licence* ___ (1989 Bond film)
48 In a fog
51 Jacksonville team, to fans
52 Sunblock ingredient
53 Pitti Palace river
54 *Good Times* producer
55 Singular
56 Cooked through
57 Bonn article
58 Spell of cold weather

★ Cage the Animals

Draw lines to completely divide up the grid into small squares with exactly one animal per square. The squares should not overlap.

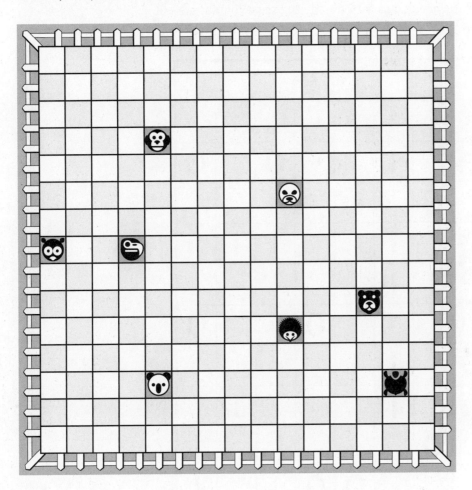

DOODLE PUZZLE

A doodle puzzle is a combination of images, letters and/or numbers that represent a word or a concept. If you cannot solve a doodle puzzle, do not look at the answer right away. Think hard—and outside the box.

5 down
4 down
3 down
2 down
1 down

★★ Binairo

Complete the grid with zeros and ones until there are 5 zeros and 6 ones in every row and every column. No more than two of the same number can be next to or under each other. Rows or columns with exactly the same content are not allowed. There is only one valid solution.

I						I				
		I		I		0		0		
I		I	0							
				I			I	I		
			I	I			I			
					0				0	
		0		I	I					
	0			I				I		
			0						I	
0	I				0	0			I	

CHANGE ONE

Change one letter in each of these two words to form a common two-word phrase.

RUMBLE PIT

★★ Low Points by John M. Samson

ACROSS
1 "Guys only" party
5 B-complex acid
10 Panache
14 Rose in a *Music Man* song
15 False wing
16 Yoda's pupil
17 *From Here to Eternity* island
18 Of an arm bone
19 *Idomeneo* heroine
20 What Evel Knievel dreamed of making
23 South Carolina river
24 Michele of *Glee*
25 PC ports
27 Little ___ (Custer's last stand)
31 Dot in the ocean
34 Harry Potter, for one
36 New Guinea port
37 TV show hosted by Ronald Reagan
41 Major record label
42 Fast-shrinking sea
43 Icicle sites
44 Aaron's rod, at one point
47 Algerian seaport
49 "32 Flavors" singer DiFranco
50 *Dr. No* star Andress
54 Martian canyon
60 Wicked
61 Acting coach Uta
62 Wrinkly tangelo
63 A flatfish
64 Puff up
65 Ward in *The Fugitive*
66 Dweeb
67 Braved the odds
68 Genesis creation

DOWN
1 Arduous travels
2 Wonder Woman's crown
3 Islamic call to prayer
4 Dress glove
5 Spigot
6 Cantina stew
7 Sally ___ bread
8 "Now ___ me down ..."
9 Wozniacki of tennis
10 *Deep Impact* star Wood
11 Tubby's cartoon chum
12 Tamiroff in *Lord Jim*
13 Lowest high tide
21 3-D feature
22 Not pos.
26 Begin
27 Maria in *Coyote Ugly*
28 Fifth king of Norway
29 Collin of Nashville
30 Capone's nemesis
31 "Beware the ___ of March!"
32 Star-dotted
33 Dragon's den
35 Guido's high note
38 Dropped off the radar
39 Ache
40 Ballerina
45 Bed of straw
46 Opposite of WSW
48 Bankrupt
51 Egged on
52 Charles de Gaulle's birthplace
53 Afghan or Thai, e.g.
54 Sleeveless wear
55 Asseverate
56 Von Shtupp in *Blazing Saddles*
57 ___ fide (in bad faith)
58 Petri-dish gel
59 Fibrous network

★ BrainSnack®—Fall Colors

How many different types of trees are in the forest?

BLOCK ANAGRAM

Form the words that are described in the brackets with the letters above the grid. Extra letters are already in the right place.

SENEGAL (U.S. city)

★ Cars

All the words are hidden vertically, horizontally or diagonally—in both directions. The letters that remain unused form a sentence from left to right.

```
R I N C R D R A O B H S A D N
O E T A R S B U M P E R I N O
O W H E E L L G L G N I N U T
D H G Y D Y E S T R T R I M S
I E I D N S S C T E R U O E I
N E L O I V E C O U P É R H P
I L E B L N I K R C R O N B P
M S K E Y N D T A O L H A E O
L L A A C G W I T R A U D S F
M I R R O R A A C N B A T O R
C E B C A R I B D A L C M C A
N U F A C D T L R S T O U R H
E R S T A O E L O I O O K F O
S P A R K P L U G R A L R A L
T E R N A S T L E B T A E S T
I V T A E S K C A B E N S O U
R P M A L G O F C E S T O F E
N E T H E A D L I G H T R G Y
```

CYLINDER
DASHBOARD
DIESEL
DOOR
FOG LAMP
HANDLE
HEADLIGHT
HORN
INDICATORS
MIRROR
PEDALS
PISTON
RADIATOR
RIMS
SEAT
SEAT BELT
SPARK PLUG
TUNING
TURBO
WHEEL
WHEELS

AIRBAG
BACK SEAT
BODY

BRAKE LIGHT
BRAKES
BUMPER

CLUTCH
COOLANT
COUPÉ

FRIENDS

What do the following words have in common?

CRANIAL CURRICULAR LOGICAL MARITAL VASCULAR VEHICULAR

★★ High Points by John M. Samson

ACROSS

1 *Do the Right Thing* pizzeria
5 Sandbar
10 Annual melt
14 Hic, ___, hoc
15 "California, ___ come ..."
16 McGowan of *Charmed*
17 Commedia dell'___
18 Windows font
19 Utah resort
20 Highest peak in New Hampshire
23 Break open
24 Polynesian dish
25 City on the Ural
27 Ripped off
31 Skimp
34 Sarah Brightman album
36 Battery size
37 Colorado gold rush slogan
41 *Fables in Slang* author
42 Feminine noun suffix
43 "___ My Head": Ashlee Simpson
44 Use a ruler
47 Hot tubs
49 Sounds from 47 Across
50 Abrade
54 Cut and run
60 *Camelot* character
61 "Oh, ___ don't!"
62 Faculty head
63 Glittering vein
64 "Plant ___ and watch it grow"
65 *High Road to China* heroine
66 Strategy
67 Will Rogers prop
68 TVs

DOWN

1 SeaWorld orca
2 Composer Copland
3 ___ *Now Praise Famous Men*
4 Broadway opener
5 Garments for granny
6 Olympus queen
7 Troublemaking goddess
8 Jacob's first wife
9 Manila man
10 Calamitous
11 Laura of *Remington Steele*
12 Referring to
13 Start on solids
21 Baker's dozen?
22 Persona ___ grata
26 *Nancy Drew* author
27 Chinese lap dogs
28 ___ monde (high society)
29 Sunrise locale
30 *Enterprise* android
31 Cyber junk mail
32 Bay of Fundy attraction
33 Home-furnishings chain
35 Aykroyd in *Ghostbusters*
38 Confidential
39 "La Cucaracha" subject
40 Greyhound trips
45 Bring down
46 "Weird Al" Yankovic movie
48 Bogus
51 An analgesic
52 Braid
53 Anglo-Saxon laborers
54 Beatles album
55 Hydroxyl compound
56 "Another Pyramid" musical
57 "Horse Fair" painter Bonheur
58 Mast chains
59 Attacks weeds

★★ Keep Going

Start on a blank square of your choice and connect as many blank squares as possible with one single continuous line. You can only connect squares along vertical and horizontal lines, not along diagonal lines. You must continue the connecting line up until the next obstacle, i.e. the rim of the box, a black square or a square that has already been used. You can change direction at any obstacle you meet. Each square can only be used once. The number of blank squares that will be left unused is marked in the upper square. There is more than one solution. We only show one solution.

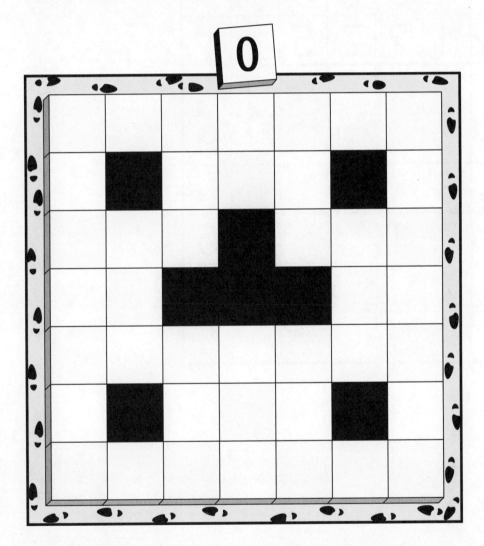

REPOSITION PREPOSITION

Unscramble OWN CHAIR ACCIDENT and find a three-word preposition.

★★ Sudoku

Fill in the grid so that each row, each column and each 3 x 3 frame contains every number from 1 to 9.

	9			5	8	7		4
5	7	1		3	9	8		
6		4	1	2	7	5		
7		5				1		
4	1							9
			3					
		8		1				5
	4		7					
				9				

SANDWICH

What four-letter word belongs between the word at left and the word at right, so that the first and second word, and the second and third word, each form a common compound word or phrase?

FRIEND _ _ _ _ WRECK

★★ Entomology Exam I by Karen Peterson

ACROSS

1 Hearty companion
5 "Purple People Eater" singer Wooley
9 Prior's superior
14 *La Fille Perdue* playwright
15 Prefix for space
16 "I Will Be" singer Lewis
17 Five-winged pollinators
19 "Rock Me Amadeus" rocker
20 C-3PO, e.g.
21 Stays in a holding pattern
23 "Dominique" singer, for one
24 *Cats* noise
25 Hopeful one
29 Lunacy
32 Kind of fair
33 Insect stage
35 Numerical suffix
36 CBer's "I hear you"
37 Infer from data
38 Ancient cry of revelry
39 Beer
40 Igneous rock material
41 *A Fish Called Wanda* Oscar winner
42 Change the order of
44 Vice President under Hayes
46 Suffix for silver
47 *A Nightmare on ___ Street* (1984)
48 Almond candy
51 Affliction
55 Stadium path
56 Fastest insect
58 Actuate
59 Per capita
60 Shoe insert
61 Cobbler forms
62 "Can't do it, Sasha"
63 Adds turf to

DOWN

1 "Aren't we the comedian?!"
2 In a while
3 Float a loan
4 Forever and a day
5 Louisiana border river
6 Take note
7 "Able was I ___ ..."
8 Autumn pear
9 *La Traviata* lead
10 Aid to navigators
11 Cotton field pest
12 "___ I Had a Secret Love"
13 New Mexican ski resort
18 "___ the Top": Porter
22 Spin doctor's concern
25 Songwriter's org.
26 Filched
27 Yellowjacket relatives
28 Wave crest
29 Amazon parrot
30 McCartney's *Standing ___*
31 Absolute
34 Tight-lipped
37 All gone
38 Earth, wind and fire
40 Cigars pitched by Edie Adams
41 Horse of the Year (1960–64)
43 Bungstarter, e.g.
45 Asset in the NBA
48 Sandbox toy
49 Mr. Abel's bird-girl love
50 Paradise lost
51 Bait fish
52 Bushy hairdo
53 *Call of the Wild* vehicle
54 Spud buds
57 Sugar ___ Robinson

★ Word Sudoku

Complete the grid so that each row, each column and each 3 x 3 frame contains the nine letters from the black box below. The hidden nine-letter word is in the diagonal from top left to bottom right.

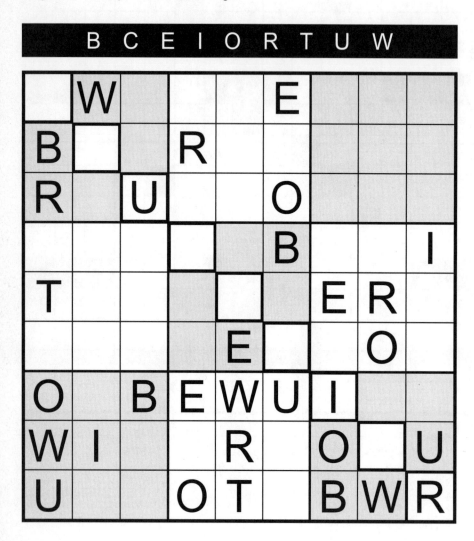

B C E I O R T U W

LETTERBLOCKS

Move the letterblocks around so that words are formed on top and below that you can associate with musical instruments.

P G R P E B I
E U A M T T P

★★★ Sport Maze

Draw the shortest way from the ball to the goal. You can only move along vertical and horizontal lines, not along diagonal lines. The figure on each square indicates the number of squares the ball must be moved in the same direction. You can change direction at each stop.

1	5	3	4	4	4
1	2		4	2	1
4	3	3	1	4	4
4	2	1	3	4	2
1	2	4	3	1	4
2	1	5	4	1	2

DOUBLETALK

What word means "a thing" or "to protest"?

★★ Entomology Exam II by Karen Peterson

ACROSS

1 "Toodle-oo!"
5 "Hot Lips" portrayer
9 Gave a darn?
14 *A God in Ruins* author
15 "Toodle-oo!"
16 A little garlic
17 Painted lady
19 *Rodeo* composer Copland
20 Microscopic creatures
21 Alley X's
23 10-percenter
24 Fondue ingredient
25 Esteemed
29 "Twenty Questions" category
32 Henhouse perch
33 Long-armed pongid
35 Chowed down
36 Gloaming
37 Pickling solution
38 In good time
39 *H.M. Pulham, ___:* Marquand
40 Show of *Melrose Place*
41 Playwright Chekhov
42 Noncommittal
44 Broad political pardon
46 "___ All the Way Home" (1959 hit)
47 Keyboard key
48 Agent's clientele
51 Compass points?
55 Aerial stunts
56 Fastest running insect
58 Roman burial stone
59 Asia's shrinking sea
60 "___ Swell": Rodgers & Hart
61 Arid refuges
62 Jackass remark
63 White-tailed eagle

DOWN

1 Symphonic instrument
2 Jack-in-the-pulpit
3 Ex-Giant Fuentes
4 Phone button
5 Abrade
6 Better half
7 Ending for editor
8 Petite poodles
9 Haunted house job?
10 Lily maid of Astolat
11 Busy formicary denizens
12 Ancient cry of revelry
13 Scout units
18 Film critic Roger
22 Bale binder
25 *As You Like It* forest
26 Dip into water
27 Most dangerous insects
28 Miami golf resort
29 Big ray
30 On ___ (carousing)
31 "Fly Away" singer Kravitz
34 "When oysters ___ season"
37 Arctic goose
38 Amusing tale
40 Bermuda and bamboo, for two
41 Snow goose genus
43 Extra-base hit
45 In a timid way
48 Additionally
49 *La Dolce Vita* composer
50 Worker at a walkout
51 Campus sports org.
52 *The Wizard of Oz* star
53 Course for an MBA: Abbr.
54 Elisabeth in *Leaving Las Vegas*
57 "Bobby Hockey"

★★★ BrainSnack®—Star Gazer

Which star (1-12) is not the correct color?

TRANSADDITION

Add one letter to TRAILS NUT and rearrange the rest to find a connection.

★ Sudoku Twin

Fill in the grid so that each row, each column and each 3 x 3 frame contains every number from 1 to 9. A sudoku twin is two connected 9 x 9 sudokus.

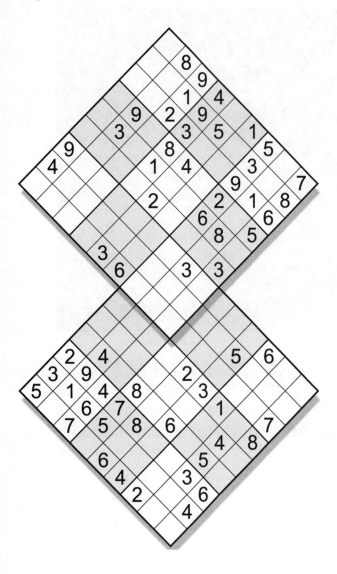

BLOCK ANAGRAM

Form the word that is described in the brackets with the letters above the grid. Extra letters are already in the right place.

CANNOT CUT (someone who audits business)

A									

★★ 2011 Chart-Toppers by Michele Sayer

ACROSS

1 Carpet line
5 *1776* protagonist
10 Chi followers
14 *Brokeback Mountain* heroine
15 Steel-collar worker
16 "Be quiet!"
17 "Do not change," to an editor
18 Associate of Souter
19 "En garde!" weapon
20 Blake Shelton hit
22 UTEP team
24 C-3PO, e.g.
25 Party gift
26 Ethnic Zambian
27 Moody Blues album
30 "Solve or spin" sayer
33 Ancient Germanic invaders
34 Orinoco tributary
35 12th Hebrew month
36 Watergate evidence
37 1040 IDs
38 Bradley and Begley
39 Sobbed
40 All over the place
41 Broiler rooms
43 *A Thousand Clowns* director
44 Domains
45 *Roseanne* actor John
49 *Jeopardy!* contestants, e.g.
51 OneRepublic hit
52 "___ Appeal": Babyface
53 Appropriate
55 Slaughter of baseball
56 ___ majesty
57 Hair tint
58 Glaswegian
59 Smart-mouth
60 Lawn tool
61 Volleyball stats

DOWN

1 Alexander of *NCIS*
2 "Bennie and the Jets" singer John
3 *FoxTrot* cartoonist
4 Cloth
5 *Aladdin* setting
6 Allotted
7 Anne Nichols hero
8 Bit of cleverness
9 Bears
10 Amazing up-and-comer
11 Nicki Minaj hit
12 Czech river
13 "___ Leaving Home": Beatles
21 Tempera base
23 Currier's partner
25 Threw a party for
27 Dummies
28 Pacific eagles
29 Optimistic
30 Look for
31 Walmart rival
32 Lady Antebellum hit
33 Market upticks
36 Blackbeard buried it
37 Like some grapes
39 "A Song for the Lonely" singer
40 Disposition
42 Blini brothers
43 Chris in *Seabiscuit*
45 Rough at St. Andrews
46 Chop
47 "The game is ___": Holmes
48 "Cheep" homes?
49 Belt hole makers
50 Citi Field predecessor
51 ___-ho
54 Crosby of hockey

★★ Sunny Weather

Where will the sun shine knowing that each arrow points in the direction of a spot where the symbol is located? The symbols cannot be next to each other vertically, horizontally or diagonally. A symbol cannot be placed on top of an arrow. We show one symbol.

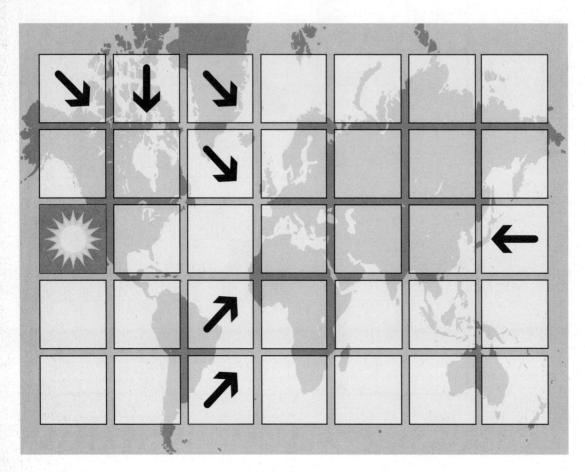

BLOCK ANAGRAM

Form the word that is described in the brackets with the letters above the grid. Extra letters are already in the right place.

POOL TABLE FLY (athlete)

| | | | | | A | | | | | | | | R |

★ Word Pyramid

Each word in the pyramid has the letters of the word above it, plus a new letter.

A
(1) Babylonian god of wisdom
(2) large body of salt water
(3) occasion for buying at reduced prices
(4) rent
(5) benumbed
(6) get worse
(7) delight

MISSING LETTER PROVERB

Fill in each missing letter, indicated by an X, to make a well-known proverb.

XLX XOOX XXINXS MXST XOME XO AX XND

★ Cage the Animals

Draw lines to completely divide up the grid into small squares with exactly one animal per square. The squares should not overlap.

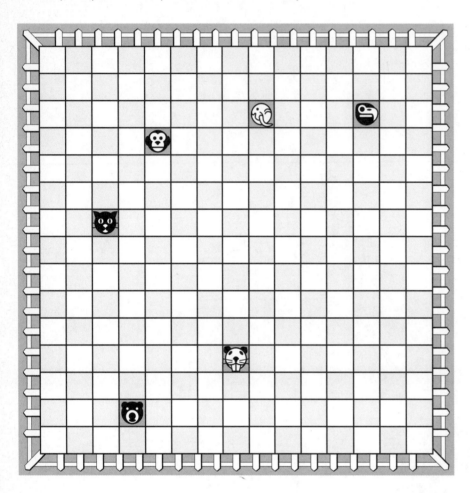

END GAME

The words you are seeking all have the letters END in them in the position indicated.
When you have found all of the answers, from the clues on the right, one column will reveal the END GAME word and give you a shade.

_	_	_	E	N	D	_	_	Meant
_	_	_	_	E	N	D	_	_	Sociable
_	E	N	D	_	_	_	_	Flexible
_	_	_	E	N	D	_	_	Abandoned

★★ Actor and Actress by Peggy O'Shea

ACROSS

1 Cheryl of *Charlie's Angels*
5 Portuguese ___-war
10 E Indian tourist spot
14 Russian range
15 Tedium
16 Competed
17 Editor Talese et al.
18 Witherspoon in *Walk the Line*
19 "A" in code
20 Game with wickets
22 Brooklyn streetcar, once
24 "Bam!" chef
25 *Sister Act* vocal group
26 *From Russia With Love* actress
28 George ___ Shaw
30 Botched it
32 "Mona Lisa" feature
34 Long in *Boiler Room*
35 Activity in a virtual room
36 Able to come back quickly
37 Hogwarts graduation gift
38 Drive away
39 Slice thinly
40 "Correct!"
41 Ceremonially impure
43 Almost boil
45 Chosen few
46 Dahl in *Watch the Birdie*
49 Helen Hunt film
51 Firedog
52 Like 5.1 surround
53 Chamber-music instrument
55 *After the Thin Man* dog
56 Skinny
57 Inlay
58 Publisher Zuckerman
59 Visualized
60 Mrs. Gorbachev
61 *Mikado* blade

DOWN

1 Picador's weapon
2 1960s band Strawberry ___ Clock
3 *Harry Potter and the Deathly Hallows* actor
4 Circumspect
5 Nothing more than
6 Old-time dill
7 112.5 degrees from W
8 Force from office
9 With angry intensity
10 Toyota sedan
11 *The X-Files* actress
12 Alluding (to)
13 "Rome wasn't built in ___"
21 Compassionate
23 Czech river
27 Afghan or Thai, e.g.
28 Takes the bait
29 Carpentry groove
30 Beige
31 Liebfraumilch, e.g.
33 *Jersey Shore* network
36 "Anything you say"
37 *The Rose Tattoo* playwright
39 Faction
40 Sonneteer
42 Cut
44 Land of seven time zones
47 Dame of South Bend?
48 Maternal relative
49 "Now hear ___!"
50 W.H. Hudson's bird girl
51 Pale brews
54 Keikogi belt

★ Binairo

Complete the grid with zeros and ones until there are 6 zeros and 6 ones in every row and every column. No more than two of the same number can be next to or under each other. Rows or columns with exactly the same content are not allowed. There is only one valid solution.

	0		0								
0			I						I		
	0			I		0					
			0	I					0	0	
	I	I					I			0	
0	I							I			
						0					
	I		I		I		0		I		0
	0	0			I			I	I		I
		I		I		0		I	I		I

LETTER LINE

Put a letter in each of the squares below to make a word which means "to take from." These numbered clues refer to other words which can be made from the whole.

1 8 4 10 COFFEE SHOP; 9 2 3 5 1 6 PICK ME UPS; 4 8 7 10 9 6 ASPECTS; 7 2 3 7 5 6 10 SHORT.

1	2	3	4	5	6	7	8	9	10

★★ Keep Going

Start on a blank square of your choice and connect as many blank squares as possible with one single continuous line. You can only connect squares along vertical and horizontal lines, not along diagonal lines. You must continue the connecting line up until the next obstacle, i.e. the rim of the box, a black square or a square that has already been used. You can change direction at any obstacle you meet. Each square can only be used once. The number of blank squares that will be left unused is marked in the upper square. There is more than one solution. We only show one solution.

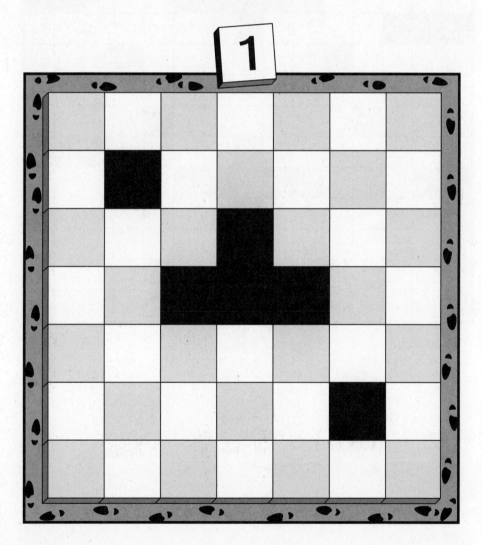

DELETE ONE

Delete one letter from INSTANCES and rearrange the rest to find elders.

★★ Best in Show by Peggy O'Shea

ACROSS

1 Ornery one
5 Impede
10 Cool guys
14 However, to texters
15 "Tag! ___ it!"
16 Hawaiian gala
17 2002 Westminster Best in Show winner
20 Filofax
21 Natives
22 European finch
23 "Can't Help Lovin' ___ Man"
24 One not yet a marquis
27 Spotted wildcats
31 Tiny amounts
34 Hubbub
36 2011 animated film
37 2010 Westminster Best in Show winner
40 Glen ___ Scotch
41 Iron shortage
42 Bridge side
43 More shabby
45 ___-raspberry juice
47 Certain trophy
48 Holiday numbers
52 Nappies
56 Stay longer than
58 2007 Westminster Best in Show winner
60 "Like ___ I go to find my fawn": Shak.
61 McAfee target
62 Hence
63 Cat with ear tufts
64 Pakistani coin
65 Like Frost's woods

DOWN

1 Freebies
2 Helpful
3 *Titanic* finder
4 Glossy to the max
5 Computer storage unit
6 Sullen look
7 ___ *Man in Havana*: Greene
8 Algonquin language
9 Didn't toss
10 Like some cell growth
11 Assembly rooms
12 Baby powder
13 Hauls into court
18 *Black Beauty* writer Sewell
19 Worrywart's words
25 Lorelei's river
26 Ne'er-do-well
27 Pertaining to vision
28 Prove innocent
29 Rail supports
30 Ilk
31 General ___ chicken
32 Four roods
33 Twelve-sided figure
35 Elec. unit
38 Chiang Kai-shek's capital
39 Celebrated
44 Two-family dwelling
46 Prefix for freeze
49 Tidal bore
50 Sovereign
51 Barber's leather
52 Business arrangement
53 Snowboarding stunt
54 Reply
55 Actor LaBeouf
56 Work with a number
57 Heavenly bear
59 ___ Lanka

★★★ BrainSnack®—Seedless

100% pure Burgundian grape juice, made from grape pulp, consists of the following percentages of water, sugars, tannin, acids, cellulose and minerals in order from top to bottom. Which percentage is wrong?

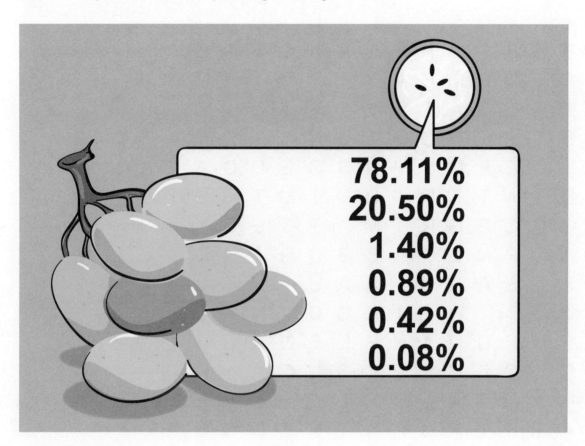

78.11%
20.50%
1.40%
0.89%
0.42%
0.08%

SQUIRCLES

Place consonants in the squares and vowels in the circles and form words in each vertical column. The definitions of the words you are looking for are listed. (The grid will reveal a the names of two animals.)

1 Give away
2 Nut
3 Expose to air
4 First event
5 Cold
6 Vote
7 Not fully developed
8 Engraved

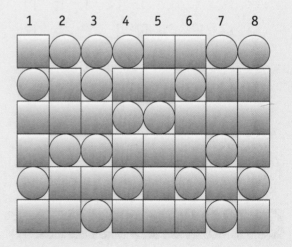

★ Mathematics

All the words are hidden vertically, horizontally or diagonally—in both directions. The letters that remain unused form a sentence from left to right.

```
N I N M O S T E L A N G U A G
A E E S T S H E D A W O T R D
R F V O R M C A X I T H I E M
B A N E G A T I V E V T G I C
E S I R R S O E T D N I I E R
G I C E E M V V N S O E D D A
L D I W T F R I U O I M T H E
A C G O E G R T M A T T E E K
B W O P M L O A B B C R A R D
O S L S A C L V E A U I M T L
D Á U T I H I I R C D A N A S
Y È M R D N A R P U E N R O W
P R O O F H E E C S D G A I C
C M A R G A I D H L E L E M E
M A T R I X C A N T E E N S S
C I E X P O N E N T N E I N C
E K N Y T I N I F N I O L W L
E D G E O R L E A R L N I N G
```

CONIC
COSINE
DEDUCTION
DERIVATIVE
DIAGRAM
DIAMETER
DIGIT
DIVIDE
ELLIPSE
EVEN
EXPONENT
INFINITY
INTEGRAL
LINE
LINEAR
LOGIC
MATRIX
NEGATIVE
NUMBER
POWER
PROOF
STATISTICS
SURFACE
TRIANGLE

ABACUS	ALGEBRA	BODY
ADD	AXIOM	CIRCLE

ONE LETTER LESS OR MORE

The word on the right side contains the letters of the word on the left side plus or minus the letter in the middle. One letter is already in the right place.

| C | A | N | O | E | I | N | G | +R | | | N | | | | | |

★★ Business Barons I by John M. Samson

ACROSS

1 Pack down
5 Frozen dessert
10 Attention-getters
14 Beam in a bridge
15 Adams and Brickell
16 *From Here to Eternity* island
17 FOX News Channel president
19 Neverland pirate
20 Bring up to speed
21 Distant
23 Longing
24 Green Jedi master
25 Wine prefix
27 "It's about time!"
30 Permeate
33 Buoyant wood
35 Confucian truth
36 Honoree's place
37 Greyhound station
38 Berlin product
39 Cockney inferno
40 Skinflint
41 AFT president Weingarten
42 TV's ___ *Place*
44 Antiquing device
46 Rowlands in *Tony Rome*
47 Crude calculator
51 Eve Titus mouse
54 Roll response
55 *Mon Oncle* star
56 Former Chrysler CEO
58 Property claim
59 Sumatran simian
60 Cultivate
61 "As Time Goes By" requester
62 From bad to ___
63 Helm position

DOWN

1 Frazzled
2 Residence
3 Wise man
4 Priceless
5 Defeated
6 Jon Arbuckle's pet
7 "Cool" amount
8 Burrito filling
9 Aldous Huxley, for one
10 Yankee catcher Jorge
11 Walmart founder
12 Elvsted in *Hedda Gabler*
13 Chop ___
18 Street show
22 Ellen ___ Barkin
26 Pudgy plus
27 *La Traviata* mezzo
28 Queen Maud ___
29 Bear or Berra
30 Aforementioned
31 Like drone bees
32 Microsoft cofounder
34 Gorilla
37 Deny
38 Florida circus town
40 Kissing disease
41 Renaissance fiddle
43 Optic membrane
45 Carport alternative
48 DeMille of Hollywood
49 "Enough already!"
50 Banal
51 *Volsunga Saga* king
52 Lunula locale
53 Architect Saarinen
54 ATM necessities
57 "... silk purse out of a sow's ___"

★★ Number Cluster

Complete the grid by constituting adjoining clusters that consist of as many cubes as the number on the cubes. At cube 5, for instance, you will have to make a five-cube cluster. Two or more figure cubes of the same value belong to the same cluster. You can only place your cubes along horizontal and/or vertical lines.

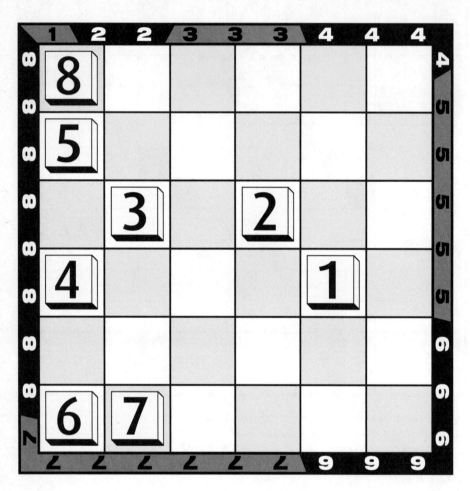

UNCANNY TURN

Rearrange the letters of the phrase to form a cognate anagram, one which is related or connected in meaning to the original phrase. The answer can be one or more words.

THEY SEE

★★ BrainSnack®—Skewered

A sausage costs half as much as a meatball and a beef cube costs twice as much as a meatball. The entire package costs $16.20. How much does a sausage cost?

DOODLE PUZZLE

A doodle puzzle is a combination of images, letters and/or numbers that represent a word or a concept. If you cannot solve a doodle puzzle, do not look at the answer right away. Think hard—and outside the box.

★★ Business Barons II by John M. Samson

ACROSS
1 "Thou ___ not kill"
6 Sun Valley lift
10 Puma and lynx
14 Abates
15 Essen article
16 Las Vegas casino
17 MacDowell in *Groundhog Day*
18 Apple cofounder
20 Cape Cod locale, familiarly
22 Avoids the big wedding
23 Blizzard condition
24 Art mart
25 *La Bohème* setting
27 "Boola Boola" singer
28 Great Plains tribe
29 Apple attachments
31 Dillydally
35 White House URL suffix
36 Outback ratite
37 Yoko ___
38 Crude cartel?
40 *Zorba the Greek* setting
42 Concerning
43 "Blue" singer Rimes
45 Still in the box
47 Takes to a higher court
50 Like tostadas
51 Like diner spoons?
52 November winners
55 Google cofounder
57 City ENE of Essen
58 Singer Brickell
59 ___-Pei dog
60 Hurricanes do this to beaches
61 Snitched
62 Porky's remark
63 First American saint

DOWN
1 Cotton on a stick
2 *The English Patient* heroine
3 Intel cofounder
4 Free time
5 Nagana carrier
6 Petulant
7 Mouthful
8 Brittany burro
9 Blows the lid off
10 Blandished
11 Soap-on-___
12 River of Rome
13 Smart-mouthed
19 She outwrestled Thor
21 ABA members: Abbr.
24 A to Z
25 Energetic
26 Perched upon
27 Oman neighbor
30 Aquatic birds
32 Electronic Data Systems founder
33 Feed the kitty
34 *A Few ___ Men* (1992)
39 Got over the bar
40 Cousteau's ship
41 Seine tributary
42 Spartan
44 No-brainer
46 Specialized markets
47 Shoelace tag
48 Home of "The Clothed Maja"
49 Hazard
50 Paper pusher
52 Susan who was Belle
53 "Inner" prefix
54 Spotted
56 Hawaiian tuna

★★★ Sport Maze

Draw the shortest way from the ball to the goal. You can only move along vertical and horizontal lines, not along diagonal lines. The figure on each square indicates the number of squares the ball must be moved in the same direction. You can change direction at each stop.

1	4	5	5	4	4
2	4	4	2	4	2
4	1	3	2	4	4
1	4	2	3		5
1	2	1	4	3	3
3	4	3	5	4	3

CHANGE ONE

Change one letter in each of these two words to form a common two-word phrase.

GREED BINGERS

★ Word Sudoku

Complete the grid so that each row, each column and each 3 x 3 frame contains the nine letters from the black box below. The hidden nine-letter word is in the diagonal from top left to bottom right.

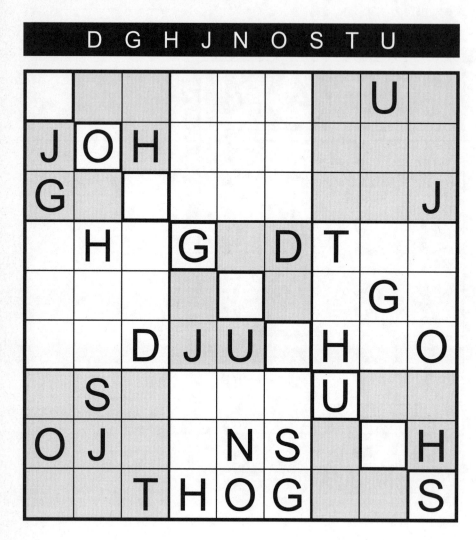

LETTERBLOCKS

Move the letterblocks around so that words are formed on top and below that you can associate with gardens.

C O S S L T O
B M P O O M S

★★ Themeless by John McCarthy

ACROSS

1 *B.C.* character Clumsy ___
5 *The Communist Manifesto* is one
10 Barely open
14 Money-changer's fee
15 Tittle-tattle
16 *Finding ___* (2003)
17 Splinter group
18 "So long, mon ami!"
19 Striped antelopes
20 Embellish
22 Linebacker's squad
24 "The Thinker," for one
25 Run counter to
26 Celtics guard Rajon
28 1984 Steve Martin film
30 Underworld
32 *Battle Cry* director Walsh
34 Electric fish
35 Pushup pushers
36 Band of fighters
37 Cubesmith Rubik
38 "Da Crime Family" rap trio
39 "Gare Saint-Lazare" painter
40 16th-century violin
41 Big Brother and the ___ Company
43 Tori Spelling's dad
45 *Friendship 7* passenger
46 Heavily satirical
49 *Please Don't Eat the ___* (1960)
51 Wisconsin capital
52 *A Loss of Roses* playwright
53 Jeweler's weight
55 Syracuse U. mascot
56 *The Lion King* baddie
57 Swap
58 *Cheers* accountant
59 *Daily Planet* reporter
60 Savants
61 *Mikado* blade

DOWN

1 *Boston Legal* matters
2 *Entourage* job
3 He played Burt on *Soap*
4 Fish chowder ingredients
5 Outlined
6 Uncouth
7 "___ in Love?"
8 Like Vassar
9 Devoted
10 *Measure for Measure* deputy
11 *Along Came Polly* star
12 Beer and skittles
13 *Titanic* heroine
21 *Black Narcissus* characters
23 Plummeted
27 Rue Morgue murderer
28 *Fantastic Voyage* carrier
29 Beautiful Wells race
30 "Thirty days ___ September ..."
31 Overbearing pride
33 Fruity quaff
36 Bonds
37 Mariah Carey hit
39 Skimpy skirt
40 Adjective for Death Valley
42 *The English Patient* setting
44 Becomes less strong
47 ___-Dame de Paris
48 Aphorism
49 "Slipped" backbone part
50 "___ Smile": Hall & Oates
51 Forced
54 Joplin's "Maple Leaf ___"

★★★ Sudoku

Fill in the grid so that each row, each column and each 3 x 3 frame contains every number from 1 to 9.

5		2	4	6	8		3	
			9		3		4	2
3					2			
6		7	2		9			8
2		4		7		3		
		3	8					7
		9	3					
7						5		
				8			6	

FRIENDS

What do the following words have in common?

BASE GENETIC GRAM LOG METER PAUSE PHONE TRIBE

★★★ BrainSnack®—Multiplier

Assuming the answers of the previous multiplications are correct, what is the answer of the last calculation?

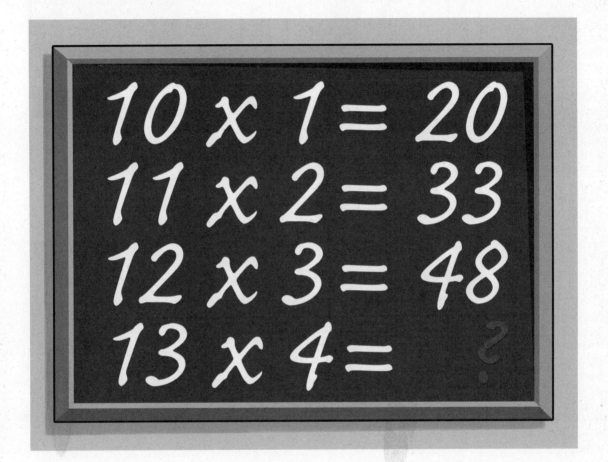

$$10 \times 1 = 20$$
$$11 \times 2 = 33$$
$$12 \times 3 = 48$$
$$13 \times 4 = \text{?}$$

SANDWICH

What five-letter word belongs between the word at left and the word at right, so that the first and second word, and the second and third word, each form a common compound word or phrase?

FINGER _ _ _ _ _ MAKER

★★★ 2011 Hit Songs by Michele Sayer

ACROSS

1 "Deal!"
5 Hogwarts study
10 "Got it!"
14 *Aida* backdrop
15 Man of Qum
16 Skyrocket
17 Airline to Lod
18 Baker's 13
19 Large swallow
20 Paisley/Underwood hit
22 À la Felix Unger
24 Bram Stoker vampire
25 Nintendo plumber
26 Burgundy burro
27 Voice of Buzz
   Lightyear
30 Drying ovens
33 Wine grape
34 Eggs
35 Hint
36 Add a lane
37 Folksinger Burl
38 Aaron's mount
39 "It's Only a ___ Moon"
40 Posed to propose
41 Makes it go
43 104, literally
44 Teaching
45 Asserted without
   proof
49 *Das Lied von der Erde*
   composer
51 Britney Spears hit
52 Home to most Indians
53 Popeye's creator
55 Hang a left
56 Fuzz
57 Booth or stand
58 S-shaped molding
59 *A Loss of Roses*
   playwright
60 Dyed-___-wool
61 Fibrous network

DOWN

1 Edgar Bergen dummy
2 Edmonton puckster
3 Alpaca relative
4 Dainty
5 Belly
6 Coffee brewing, e.g.
7 Long look
8 Opal ending
9 Apple pie spice
10 Rail at
11 Lil Wayne hit
12 Spinnaker
13 *Animal House* party
21 *Black Narcissus*
   characters
23 Pound's "___ Hora"
25 UMW member
27 Neap and ebb
28 Robbie Knievel's dad
29 *Condé ___ Traveler*
30 Dos cubed
31 "Awop-bop-a-loo-mop
   ___-bam-boom"
32 Miguel hit
33 Lab tube
36 Do a lake sport
37 M's Q, for one
39 Windex target
40 Artisan's furnace
42 Sympathize
43 *2001: A Space Odyssey*
   author
45 Overflowing
46 Assess
47 Snowy bird
48 "Thank you" speaker,
   often
49 Niger neighbor
50 Z ___ zebra
51 "___ Rhythm"
54 German article

★ Spot the Differences

Find the nine differences in the image on the right.

LETTERBLOCKS

Move the letterblocks around so that words are formed on top and below that you can associate with mistakes.

R L U B N D E
R L O B O P E

★★ Binairo

Complete the grid with zeros and ones until there are 5 zeros and 6 ones in every row and every column. No more than two of the same number can be next to or under each other. Rows or columns with exactly the same content are not allowed. There is only one valid solution.

0			0							
	0		0							
1							0	0		
		1				0				
1				0		0			0	
							1			
	0		0							0
					0			0		
	1						1			
		1			0		1		1	
		1				1			0	

DOUBLETALK

What word means "a topic" or "to cause to undergo"?

★ Cage the Animals

Draw lines to completely divide up the grid into small squares with exactly one animal per square. The squares should not overlap.

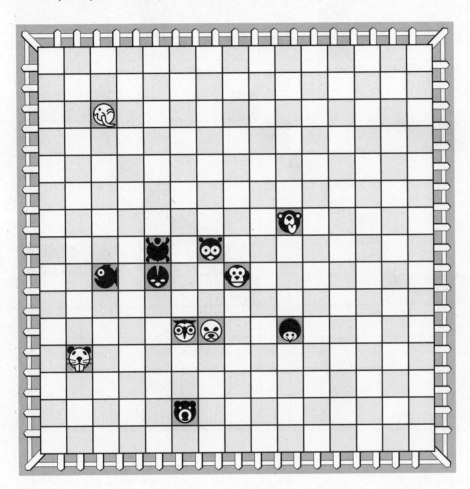

REPOSITION PREPOSITION

Unscramble HALF OF BONE and find a three-word preposition.

★★★ Themeless by Cindy Wheeler

ACROSS

1 "Isn't that ___ much?"
5 Baron Cohen in *Borat*
10 A sound from the tower
14 All dried out
15 iPad letters
16 Jamaican tangelo
17 Stravinsky ballet
18 Twenty, in Paris
19 "Heads I win, tails you ___"
20 *Fear and Loathing in Las Vegas* author
23 Arched shoe parts
24 Spicy tea
25 Green lights
26 Rather brief
30 Swiss capital
33 They come in drops
34 Greene of *The Godfather*
35 Indonesia's ___ Islands
36 "Bon appétit!"
37 Southern California valley
38 Country singer McGraw
39 Better balanced
40 It runs in a taxi
41 Beyond gaunt
43 Hawaii's Mauna ___
44 Horse for Lawrence
45 Airborne weapon
49 1956 Elvis Presley hit
53 "___ Breaky Heart"
54 *Fantastic Voyage* carrier
55 *Avatar* humanoids
56 "Long-running" suffix
57 Deli cheese
58 Tavern tipples
59 Hades river
60 Ho-hum feeling
61 Folk knowledge

DOWN

1 Japanese brewery
2 "We've Only Just ___"
3 Jeremy in *Betrayal*
4 12:50
5 French porcelain
6 Off-kilter
7 "Got other plans, sorry"
8 Seat with a tray
9 Valved brass instrument
10 Jack-in-the-___
11 Big heads
12 To boot
13 Creditor's claim
21 Sommer in *A Shot in the Dark*
22 Father of Remus
26 Jason in *Bad Teacher*
27 "You're looking at him!"
28 ___ *Like It Hot* (1959)
29 Homophone of air
30 Baseball Hall of Fame sights
31 *CHiPS* star Estrada
32 *Ben-Hur* setting
33 *The Daily Beast* founder
36 Lexis-Nexis offering
37 Like ski resorts
39 Rockefeller Center muralist
40 Concert pit
42 Voice box
43 Southern DR Congo city
45 East China Sea island
46 *Mr. Palomar* author Calvino
47 Machine handle
48 *The First Wives Club* wife
49 Some bowlers
50 German for "genuine"
51 "Hey, sailor!"
52 CNBC anchor Burnett

★ Invest

All the words are hidden vertically, horizontally or diagonally—in both directions. The letters that remain unused form a sentence from left to right.

```
E  T  A  T  S  W  H  E  E  D  A  R  T  S  A
N  S  A  W  I  N  V  E  S  T  M  E  N  T  N
V  I  T  R  A  C  K  I  N  G  H  N  G  O  A
C  O  V  E  R  R  A  T  I  O  B  G  A  C  L
S  E  C  I  R  P  R  E  F  F  O  O  I  K  Y
E  Y  T  I  L  I  T  A  L  O  V  S  N  R  S
L  C  I  S  N  I  R  T  N  I  N  H  D  U  I
L  A  T  I  P  A  C  C  I  T  N  A  V  E  S
X  E  D  N  I  E  C  I  R  P  E  R  A  H  S
S  U  O  N  D  T  I  N  N  A  G  E  W  E  C
N  R  T  P  E  E  E  P  O  D  S  U  T  D  U
R  O  R  O  T  D  P  U  I  T  E  H  N  G  S
U  N  E  B  M  I  I  O  S  O  B  X  O  I  T
T  E  A  N  A  E  O  V  S  Y  F  O  D  N  O
E  X  S  S  O  N  R  N  I  I  A  F  N  G  D
R  T  U  E  D  E  K  T  M  D  T  H  O  D  I
E  R  R  E  B  A  Y  R  E  R  A  E  L  C  A
R  U  Y  N  N  I  Q  N  G  A  R  I  S  K  N
```

DEPOSIT
DIVIDEND
EMISSION
EURONEXT
HEDGING
INDEX
INTRINSIC
INVESTMENT
LONDON
NASDAQ
OFFER PRICE
OPTION
RETURN
RIGHT
SELL
SHARE
SHARE PRICE INDEX
STATE
STOCK
TRACKING
TRADE
TREASURY
VOLATILITY
WARRANT

ANALYSIS
BANK
BOND

BONUS
CAPITAL
CLEARER

COVER RATIO
CRASH
CUSTODIAN

TRANSADDITION

Add one letter to RENAMING REVEALS and rearrange the rest to find a connection.

★★ Sunny Weather

Where will the sun shine knowing that each arrow points in the direction of a spot where the symbol is located? The symbols cannot be next to each other vertically, horizontally or diagonally. A symbol cannot be placed on top of an arrow. We show one symbol.

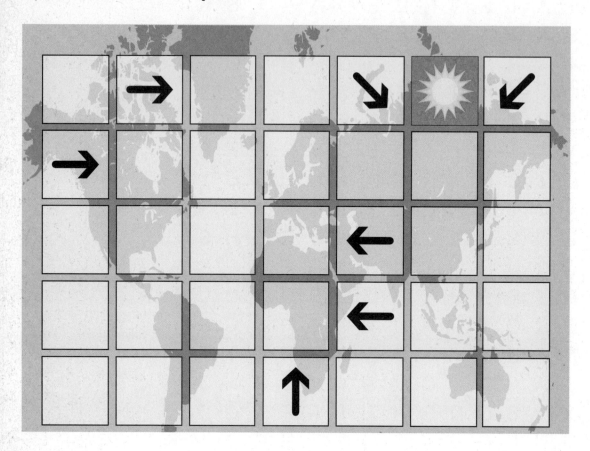

BLOCK ANAGRAM

Form the words that are described in the brackets with the letters above the grid. Extra letters are already in the right place.

LONESOME RIG (chamber)

			P							

★★★ State Birds by Cindy Wheeler

ACROSS

1 Big name in cookware
5 German art song
9 "Beat it!"
14 Prefix for drome
15 Green emotion
16 "___ in Paradise": Poe
17 State bird of Maine
19 "The Lovely" Muse
20 Legolas player Bloom
21 Adjective for a model
23 "Fore!" site
24 "Me too" sort
25 Eeyore's creator
29 Agar colony
32 ___ a Letter to My Love (1981)
33 Baseball deal
35 "Go ahead" signal
36 Caribou male
37 Something to get into
38 Tucked away
39 TV type
40 Part of a lunar cycle
41 Crime site
42 Shoreline problem
44 Rap sheets
46 "Not so fast!"
47 Dancer Lubovitch
48 Peach State capital
51 Transcend
55 Authoritative proclamation
56 State bird of New Jersey
58 Sacher cake
59 Dawn author Wiesel
60 A Plains tribe
61 Fahrenheit 451 actor Werner
62 Dog food brand
63 Attacks, puppy-style

DOWN

1 Snack with a shell
2 Oded in The Mummy
3 Nutmeg covering
4 GPS asset
5 Slow and heavy
6 Prefix for China
7 "Who's That Girl" rapper
8 Hides the gray
9 St. Patrick's spire
10 Trumpet look-alike
11 State bird of New Mexico
12 Poker stake
13 "Is it just ___ ..."
18 Genuflected
22 Magna cum ___
25 Usher's beat
26 Daisy relative
27 State bird of Kansas
28 Hawke in Great Expectations
29 Pickled bud
30 Roly-poly
31 A cube has twelve
34 Dorm police, so to speak
37 Piglet
38 Desert stinger
40 Avant-gardist
41 Flying ace Snoopy's wear
43 1999 Jake Busey sitcom
45 Loses a tail
48 Prefix for pilot
49 Ali stats
50 Like single malt Scotch
51 Snowboarded
52 Voting "no"
53 Old English poet
54 "___ a Lady": Tom Jones
57 ABBA drummer Brunkert

★★ BrainSnack®—Write Me

Which letter should replace the question mark?

END GAME

The words you are seeking all have the letters END in them in the position indicated.
When you have found all of the answers, from the clues on the right, one column will reveal the
END GAME word which is an end game in itself.

_	_	_	_	_	E	N	D		Squander
_	_	E	N	D	_	_	_		Cruel, wicked
_	E	N	D	_	_	_	_		Available as a resource
E	N	D	_	_	_	_	_		Inner layers of cells

★★ Kakuro

Each number in a black area is the sum of the numbers that you have to enter in the next empty boxes. The empty boxes that make up the sum are called a run. The sum of the across run is written above the diagonal in the black area and the sum of the down run is written below the diagonal. Runs can only contain the numbers 1 through 9 and each number in a run can only be used once. The gray boxes only contain odd numbers and the white only even numbers.

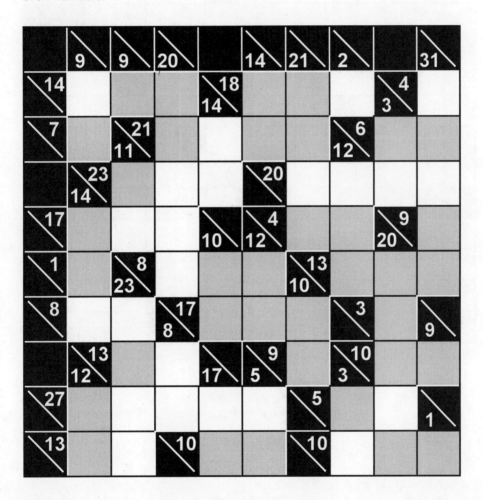

MISSING LETTER PROVERB

Fill in each missing letter, indicated by an X, to make a well-known proverb.

XAXKING XOXS XELXOM XITX

★★★ Say Cheese! by Michele Sayer

ACROSS

1 Act a bit vexed
5 Alop
10 "A" in code
14 "___ on Down the Road"
15 Office scribe
16 Welsh form of John
17 Smidgen
18 "Great blue" bird
19 Censor's concern
20 Mild cheese with an orange rind
22 Twofold
24 *Pollyanna* author Porter
25 Indira Gandhi's father
26 Book before Exod.
27 Once upon a time
30 Algonquian abode
33 Becomes wan
34 Prizm maker
35 Frau's partner
36 Larry of *Curb Your Enthusiasm*
37 Wall Street animal
38 Orinoco tributary
39 *Dragonwyck* writer Anya
40 A moving crowd
41 Penultimate month
43 "April Love" singer Boone
44 "___ Melancholy": Keats
45 "Could be"
49 Auriferous
51 Spaghetti cheese
52 Mine, in Marseilles
53 16th-century violin
55 Largest Latvian city
56 Unaccompanied
57 Urge forward
58 Major German dam
59 Two-___ sloth
60 Acts like a stallion
61 Rolltop

DOWN

1 "Cherchez la ___!"
2 *High Sierra* director Walsh
3 *Teen Wolf Too* actress Chandler
4 Hannah Montana, for one
5 Kutcher of *Two and a Half Men*
6 Texas longhorn
7 Virginia/North Carolina lake
8 Roxy Music founder
9 Pondered
10 Allay one's fears
11 Odorous German cheese
12 NBA technical
13 "Deal me in" indicator
21 Snicker-___
23 "Law" of current flow
25 *Baywatch* actress Gena
27 Act of goodwill
28 Coveted role
29 Former times
30 "Better you ___ me!"
31 Bubble Chair designer Aarnio
32 Antipasto cheese
33 Eucharist holder
36 Blithe
37 Annoyed
39 Pirate known to the Lost Boys
40 Damage
42 Circulated, in a way
43 Hazards
45 ___ Noster
46 Stage whisper
47 Beeper calls
48 "The Hunting of the ___": Carroll
49 *Atlas Shrugged* hero
50 Herman Melville book
51 Hemingway epithet
54 Spouse of M.

★★ Word Sudoku

Complete the grid so that each row, each column and each 3 x 3 frame contains the nine letters from the black box below. The hidden nine-letter-word is in the diagonal from top left to bottom right.

| A | B | E | R | S | T | U | W | Y |

T								
			B		W			
							S	
E	Y							
	A						R	B
	Y	R					A	
S					T			W
R	U	S	W	B	A			
W	B		E	A	U	T		

LETTERBLOCKS

Move the letterblocks around so that words are formed on top and below that you can associate with emotions.

★★ Keep Going

Start on a blank square of your choice and connect as many blank squares as possible with one single continuous line. You can only connect squares along vertical and horizontal lines, not along diagonal lines. You must continue the connecting line up until the next obstacle, i.e. the rim of the box, a black square or a square that has already been used. You can change direction at any obstacle you meet. Each square can only be used once. The number of blank squares that will be left unused is marked in the upper square. There is more than one solution. We only show one solution.

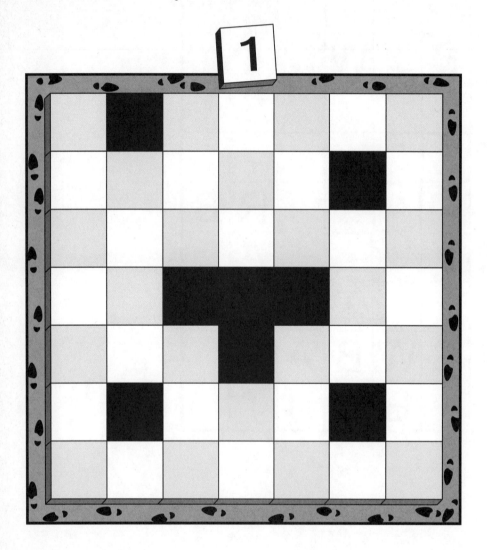

DELETE ONE

Delete one letter from USE ARMS A LOT and rearrange the rest to find a tumble?

★★★ U.S. Cities by Karen Peterson

ACROSS

1 Makes public
5 Israeli statesman Dayan
10 Take five
14 Barrymore in *Whip It*
15 At three o'clock, asea
16 Court minutes
17 Prefix meaning "all"
18 *Children of the Sun* playwright
19 Source of fiber
20 Florida's "Sunshine City"
23 Cause for court-ordered rehab
24 Bee prefix
25 Answered
29 Distinguished
33 Survey-answer choice
34 J.D. Salinger heroine
36 A fifth of DX
37 Virginia city named after King George III's wife
41 ___ *for Killer*: Grafton
42 Banana throwaway
43 "___ ears!"
44 Royal emblem
47 Settled
49 Mount where Aaron died
50 Temporary drop
51 U.S. Air Force Academy locale
60 Take too much of
61 He fails to pass the bar
62 Geese that rarely swim
63 Things on other things
64 Kiwi-shaped
65 Ovid's "it was"
66 Darjeeling and Oolong
67 4 x 4, e.g.
68 The i's have it

DOWN

1 Kerfuffles
2 Food maven Rombauer
3 "Labors of Hercules" artist
4 Con artist
5 Chatterbox
6 Hecklephone cousin
7 Spanish muralist
8 Whiting
9 Sheikhdoms
10 White Carroll creature
11 Cream shade
12 Five-pointed figure
13 Grapefruit taste
21 Play with idly
22 Whirlpool setting
25 Ice, in bar lingo
26 Value system
27 Lunar stage
28 Ward off
29 Detect a fragrance
30 Brilliant performance
31 Capital of Nord, France
32 Road sign
35 ___ Anne de Bellevue
38 Jim Croce hit
39 Chapel head
40 Not in reality
45 Telethon bank
46 Rocky top
48 Diving fisher
51 Egyptian Christian
52 Drooling dog of comics
53 *Shark Tale* dragon fish
54 Did a half gainer
55 Judy Moody's aunt
56 Bee bristle
57 Sleuth Wolfe
58 Irritating insect
59 Hardens

★★★ Sport Maze

Draw the shortest way from the ball to the goal. You can only move along vertical and horizontal lines, not along diagonal lines. The figure on each square indicates the number of squares the ball must be moved in the same direction. You can change direction at each stop.

2	1	3	4	5 (ball)	2
5	2	4	2	2	5
4	2	3	2	1	4
4	3	2	3	4	1
3	3	1	3	2	(goal)
3	1	5	2	3	2

LETTER LINE

Put a letter in each of the squares below to make a word which means "to found." These numbered clues refer to other words which can be made from the whole.

8 3 4 5 6 1 STEADFAST; 5 4 2 7 6 HERB; 2 4 6 3 CONDIMENT; 8 6 4 5 CHUNK.

1	2	3	4	5	6	7	8	9

★★★ Sudoku

Fill in the grid so that each row, each column and each 3 x 3 frame contains every number from 1 to 9.

8								
	9	1						
7							4	2
		2	4					
4				9			1	8
				1	6			
		3		6	4		9	
	1		8		9	2	5	
	4	8	5	2		6	3	

CHANGELINGS

Each of the three lines of letters below should spell words which have a legal connection. The letters have been mixed up. Four letters from the first word are now in the third line, four letters from the third word are in the second line and four letters from the second word are in the first line. The remaining letters are in their original places. What are the words?

```
I O N N E S S C E N
S L D I M T M T N T
C E T T F E I E N O
```

★★★ BrainSnack®—Kisses

Which letter should replace the question mark?

ONE LETTER LESS OR MORE

The word on the right side contains the letters of the word on the left side plus or minus the letter in the middle. One letter is already in the right place.

G R E N A D E S **+E** □ □ □ □ **G** □ □ □ □

★★★ Leading Men by Karen Peterson

ACROSS

1 "Grand" homer
5 Maureen in *McLintock!*
10 Artist Rockwell
14 Lacquered metalware
15 "Light" weapon in *Star Wars*
16 "Of course!"
17 "6 'N the Mornin'" rapper
18 Pick up the tab
19 Diner sign
20 *Tin Men* star
23 *Madama Butterfly* accessory
24 Questel who voiced Betty Boop
25 Railroad bridge
29 Daybreak
33 "Son of" in Arabic
34 Jim Carrey film
36 Poet McKuen
37 Sugar suffix
38 Track longshot
39 Rarebit ingredient
40 "1-2-3" singer Barry
41 Most attractive
45 Bronze
46 Buck feature
48 Point-getters
50 "___ tu" (Verdi aria)
51 World Cup cheer
52 *The Sopranos* star
61 Online one
62 Dummy
63 Jack in *The Rare Breed*
64 Paid attendance
65 Mother-of-pearl
66 *Hope & Faith* actress Kelly
67 Zipped along
68 Like chiffon
69 "Beautiful Girls" singer Kingston

DOWN

1 Recipe directive
2 Activity centers
3 Baldwin in *The Shadow*
4 Modus operandi
5 Big bird
6 No picnic
7 In la-la land
8 Rumble-seat locale
9 Gordon of *The Wild, Wild West*
10 *24* star Sutherland
11 "Cunning hunter" in Genesis
12 Meadowlands team
13 1979 Polanski film
21 Adjacent to
22 Pull out
25 *Twelfth Night* heroine
26 *Ghosts* playwright
27 About
28 Jamboree dwellings
29 Gurus
30 Fit to be tied
31 Green energy
32 "Lest we lose our ___": Browning
35 Gym pad
41 Mug word
42 Roots
43 *Muppet Show* stage manager
44 Turnpike charge
47 Acted like a creep, in a way
49 Alludes
52 *Mother, ___ & Speed* (1976)
53 Memo "pronto"
54 Dispense justice
55 Stage actress Menken
56 "Bravo!"
57 ___-mi (cash)
58 "Would ___ to You?": Eurythmics
59 *Falcon Crest* valley
60 Model wife of David Bowie

★ Biology

All the words are hidden vertically, horizontally or diagonally—in both directions. The letters that remain unused form a sentence from left to right.

```
B S I O E S U G N U F L S O G
Y C I S R A N K E X A G C T S
C I A F O I E I N C N E T H A
T T I O V C S N S I S O M S O
S E R S I E T S R Y L I M A F
D N E S N L U H Y M O T A N A
O E T I M L T I L U N G S I D
P G C L O W I P E S L I V T I
O E A N O A E S U A P O N E M
R R B R G L C R B E A T U R R
H O G E S L F E N D I O X I N
T V O R M L O E R E F L E X E
R I S O A M L N O I T A T U M
A N I M A L S P E C I E S F L
I R M F O O R G A N I S M E A
T A D P O L E N D S I I G N S
M C O F L E C N A T S I S E R
I F T A T I B A H E C Y C L E
```

CELL WALL
CYCLE
DIOXIN
FAMILY
FOSSIL
FUNGUS
GENETICS
GROWTH RINGS
HABITAT
KINSHIP
LUNGS
MAMMAL
MENOPAUSE
MUTATION
OMNIVORE
ORGANISM
OSMOSIS
POLLEN
REFLEX
RESISTANCE
RETINA
TADPOLE
TISSUE

AMOEBA
ANATOMY

ANIMAL SPECIES
ARTHROPODS

BACTERIA
CARNIVORE

UNCANNY TURN

Rearrange the letters of the phrase to form a cognate anagram, one which is related or connected in meaning to the original phrase. The answer can be one or more words.

PRANCED RANTING

★★★ BrainSnack®—Odd Number

Which number does not belong?

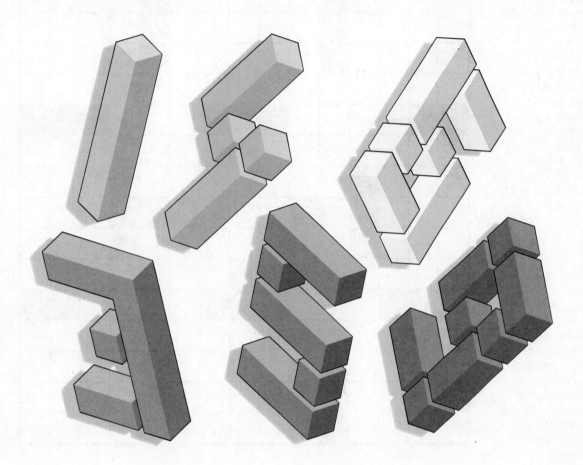

DOODLE PUZZLE

A doodle puzzle is a combination of images, letters and/or numbers that represent a word or a concept. If you cannot solve a doodle puzzle, do not look at the answer right away. Think hard—and outside the box.

★★★ This and That by John McCarthy

ACROSS

1 1040 experts
5 16th-century violin
10 "A Whiter Shade of ___"
14 *Alice Doesn't Live ___ Anymore* (1974)
15 Ancient Athenian statesman
16 Beam in a bridge
17 "... 15 miles on the ___ Canal"
18 Adult tadpoles
19 Max of *Barney Miller*
20 Deadly game in *The Deer Hunter*
23 Jacques in *Jour de fête*
24 "Here we go looby ___ ..."
25 Rolling Stones album
28 Clean dirty money
32 Camcorder button
33 Fixes
35 Cuprite, e.g.
36 Cochlea locale
37 "Callin' Me" rapper ___ Zane
38 Matchstick game
39 Lovelace in *Morning Glory*
40 Green vegetable
44 Nucleic acid
45 Advance to the rear
47 Apothecary, in London
49 Slip up
50 *7th Heaven* minister
51 Big top performer
59 Olive genus
60 Pygmy antelope
61 Mother of Romulus
62 Rents out
63 Dakota Indian
64 Counting-out word
65 Mascara target
66 Jargon
67 Applications

DOWN

1 "A Song for the Lonely" singer
2 El Misti locale
3 Patrician
4 Shilly-shally
5 Fred in *Top Hat*
6 Tide influence
7 1980s pesticide
8 Fuss and feathers
9 Cliquish
10 Bird that loves statues
11 Like ___ out of hell
12 Addition to café
13 "The Bird Cage" artist
21 Anatomical aqueduct
22 Ferrigno and Jacobi
25 Less restrictive
26 Depart
27 Fissure
28 Lavender
29 Insult comic
30 Brockovich et al.
31 Frame a second time
34 Rhone tributary
40 Spanish muralist
41 Apes
42 Reprimand (with "out")
43 Goddess of marriage
46 Beat a dead horse
48 Atmosphere
51 Emulate Big Ben
52 Endoscopy focuses
53 *As Good as It ___* (1997)
54 *Baseball Tonight* analyst Hershiser
55 Agave fiber
56 Black, in verse
57 *Stern* article
58 Florida ball club

★ Cage the Animals

Draw lines to completely divide up the grid into small squares with exactly one animal per square. The squares should not overlap.

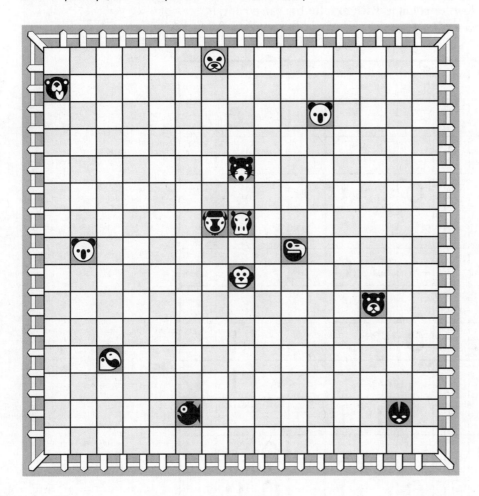

CHANGE ONE

Change one letter in each of these two words to form a common two-word phrase.

TEA CHARGE

★★★ Binairo

Complete the grid with zeros and ones until there are 6 zeros and 6 ones in every row and every column. No more than two of the same number can be next to or under each other. Rows or columns with exactly the same content are not allowed. There is only one valid solution.

	0										
									0		
	1		1								
		0		0		1	1				
1	0										
					0	0				1	
	1									1	
		1		0	0			1			
								1		1	
		1		1	1					1	
1		0					0				
			0		1		0	0			

DOODLE PUZZLE

A doodle puzzle is a combination of images, letters and/or numbers that represent a word or a concept. If you cannot solve a doodle puzzle, do not look at the answer right away. Think hard—and outside the box.

★★★ Tom, Dick and Harry by Peggy O'Shea

ACROSS

1 Apiary residents
5 Dull pains
10 Fairway hazard
14 Alcohol lamp
15 "Rush Rush" singer Abdul
16 Artful dodge
17 TOM
20 Any "Clue" character
21 Least artful
22 Sneaky chuckle
23 "Star Wars" program, for short
24 Quantico soldiers
28 Blessing
32 Roman love god
33 Blanched
35 Perjure
36 DICK
40 Did lunch
41 "___ by any other name": Shak.
42 10-stringed lute
43 Phone bug
45 Flower parts
48 *Awkward* network
49 Mano-a-mano cheer
50 Camden Yards team
54 Lydian king in 550 BC
58 HARRY
60 Sheltered, at sea
61 Mount climbed by Moses
62 Film ___
63 Lend an ear
64 Addax's big cousin
65 *A Bug's Life* bugs

DOWN

1 Porgy's love
2 Dying words from Julius
3 Seth's son
4 Blue gem
5 Army attack helicopter
6 Links rental
7 LaFayette in *Hair*
8 North Carolina college
9 Resort near Tampa
10 Tritt of country music
11 Teutonic letter
12 Plays quizmaster
13 A real pain
18 Ball-___ hammer
19 Clandestine
24 Amazon parrot
25 16th-century violin
26 Doggy name
27 Attack from above
28 Donates
29 *Family Ties* mom
30 Big name for shutterbugs
31 ___-tongue (green gentian)
34 Barry Bonds' 762: Abbr.
37 Snitch
38 Cross
39 Barry Humphries alter ego
44 Melodramatic one
46 Doughnut-shaped
47 Baseball family name
50 Aquarium beauty
51 Actor's meat
52 Virginia willow
53 Farmland
54 *Behind That Curtain* detective
55 *The Da Vinci Code* priory
56 Squad
57 Old letter opener
59 Genetic carrier

★★ Keep Going

Start on a blank square of your choice and connect as many blank squares as possible with one single continuous line. You can only connect squares along vertical and horizontal lines, not along diagonal lines. You must continue the connecting line up until the next obstacle, i.e. the rim of the box, a black square or a square that has already been used. You can change direction at any obstacle you meet. Each square can only be used once. The number of blank squares that will be left unused is marked in the upper square. There is more than one solution. We only show one solution.

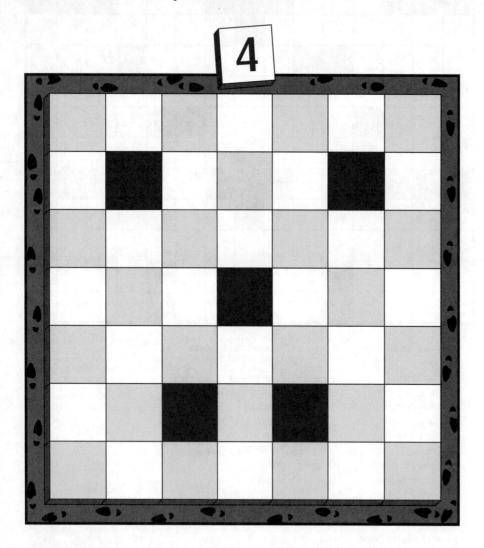

FRIENDS

What do the following words have in common?

AIR AMID APPRENTICE CITIZEN COURT FRIEND MUSICIAN

★ Word Sudoku

Complete the grid so that each row, each column and each 3 x 3 frame contains the nine letters from the black box below. The hidden nine-letter word is in the diagonal from top left to bottom right.

A B E G K L Q S Z

S					L			
		K	Q	E	S			
		E			A		B	S
Z	G		A		K			E
		S	G		L	K		
	K					G	Z	A
				A			S	L
		Q	E					
	B					Q		

SANDWICH

What five-letter word belongs between the word at left and the word at right, so that the first and second word, and the second and third word, each form a common compound word or phrase?

N E W S _ _ _ _ _ C R A F T

★★★ Cinema Classics by John M. Samson

ACROSS

1 "Breakdance" singer Irene
5 Sadistic
10 He aims for the heart
14 Penn State mascot
15 "Do I ___ Waltz?"
16 Hawaii's "Valley Isle"
17 Latin 101 verb
18 Improv joke
19 Chorale member
20 Flabby
22 Maine feline
24 Achilles ___
25 Gaseous house hazard
26 Icelandic speakers
28 Announces
30 Sudden outpouring
32 Ananias and Matilda
34 Extinct relative of 37-Across
35 Dies ___ ("Judgment Day")
36 Phone messages
37 120-pound Australians
38 "Glue" for feathers
39 "___ Eclipse of the Heart"
40 Accords
41 Purchase
43 Dig discovery
45 Audio signal receiver
46 "Dover Beach" poet
49 Leslie in Mr. Magoo
51 Like pacifists
52 Prefix meaning "eight"
53 Titanic room
55 Hawaii's state bird
56 Enterprise android
57 Pageant crown
58 Happy flower?
59 Musher's transport
60 Price for clearance
61 Dove into home

DOWN

1 Chin dimple
2 Passageway
3 Desperately Seeking Susan star
4 Raconteur's offering
5 Jacob Marley's burden
6 Foxx in Sanford and Son
7 "Friendly Skies" airline: Abbr.
8 Stonestreet of Modern Family
9 Hands
10 Mr. Spock's mother
11 A Clockwork Orange star
12 Utter
13 Warden's worry
21 It's melted in a meltdown
23 Regatta athletes
27 Be heart-pleasing
28 "From the ___ of Montezuma ..."
29 "Yo mama," e.g.
30 "Come in and ___ spell"
31 Kind of joke
33 Dockworkers' union
36 Rectifies
37 Annual report data
39 Father's Day gifts
40 Component
42 Pawn off
44 Disney's Montana
47 Maui neighbor
48 Judge played by Stallone
49 Auction bids
50 Catch red-handed
51 Affectations
54 Ovine sound

★★★ Sport Maze

Draw the shortest way from the ball to the goal. You can only move along vertical and horizontal lines, not along diagonal lines. The figure on each square indicates the number of squares the ball must be moved in the same direction. You can change direction at each stop.

2	1	5	1	4	1
3	1	4	1	3	1
1	1	1	0	1	1
5	2	3	3	2	4
5	4	4	4	3	5
	5	4	3	1	0

LETTERBLOCKS

Move the letterblocks around so that words are formed on top and below that you can associate with exercise.

F	C	E	O	T	I	B
A	S	I	N	R	S	E

★★ Sudoku X

Fill in the grid so that each row, each column and each 3 x 3 frame contains every number from 1 to 9. The two main diagonals of the grid also contain every number from 1 to 9.

9	5	4	8	7	6		3	
	1					6	4	7
2							5	
7				2				8
5	8	6	9	3		4		
		3	7				6	
					7	5		6
					4			
			8					

REPOSITION PREPOSITION

Unscramble TIP IF NOON and find a three-word preposition.

★★★ Wet Set by Karen Peterson

ACROSS

1 "Ahem!"
5 Smoothed the soil
10 Elite police unit
14 Sushi fish
15 De Becque in *South Pacific*
16 Mob boss
17 Source of tears, slangily
19 Sgt. Snorkel's dog
20 Audio systems
21 Cushiest
23 Sully
24 Feral abode
25 Facing
29 Double-deck game
32 Pearly gems
33 Track trials
35 Young socialite
36 Garden State hoop team
37 *All That Jazz* choreographer
38 Ghostly sound
39 Furor
40 Talk big
41 Look for water
42 "Jabberwocky" poet
44 Bar code machine
46 Monk's room
47 Giant of Cooperstown
48 1958 Everly Brothers hit
51 One of the Bee Gees
55 Thomas Gray poems
56 Fleshy picnic treat
58 Byrne of *Damages*
59 Berkshire jackets
60 "That ___ hay!"
61 Soprano role in *Lohengrin*
62 One of the X-Men
63 Suffix for Congo

DOWN

1 *Batman* sound effects
2 Gaiter
3 Appease
4 Updrafts
5 Edit, in a way
6 "Real Men" singer Tori
7 Champagne aperitif
8 Grand Exalted Ruler's org.
9 Abandoned
10 Nova ___
11 Cuts, in a way
12 Walk-ups: Abbr.
13 "Out of my way!" indicator
18 Keisters
22 They make waves
25 Gin mixer
26 Covent Garden production
27 V-8 Juice ingredient
28 Bar
29 Acting companies
30 Bullyrag
31 Baseball's Doubleday
34 Suffix for heir
37 Not a leader
38 Cultural center of Quebec
40 Fearless
41 Factoid
43 Waters off Port Sudan
45 Crass
48 Tiresome talker
49 Golden calf
50 Spanish cat
51 Carte du jour
52 "In a cowslip's bell ___": Shak.
53 Sing Sing residents
54 Cologne duck
57 Fit (out)

★★★ BrainSnack®—Star Tripper

The space probe has already visited four star systems in a certain order. In which order (1-4) will it visit the other systems? Answer like this: 2143.

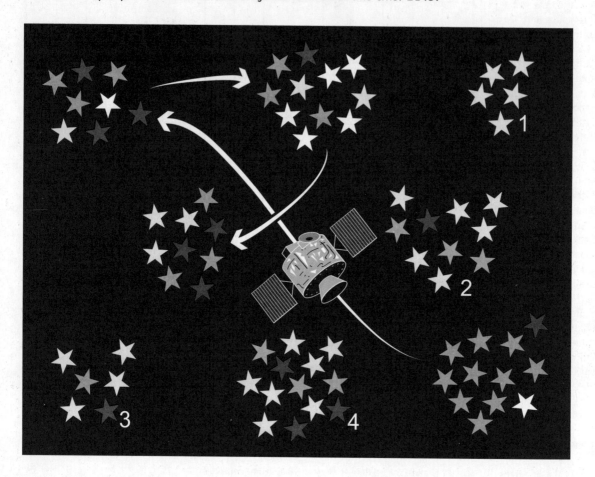

DOUBLETALK

What word means "a breeze" or "to tighten a spring"?

★ Word Pyramid

Each word in the pyramid has the letters of the word above it, plus a new letter.

M
(1) I
(2) large Australian bird
(3) donkey
(4) feather
(5) dock worker
(6) collapse or fold
(7) thin device to pluck a guitar string

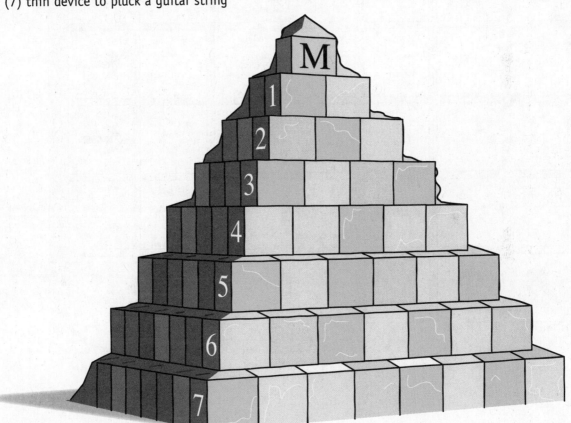

TRANSADDITION

Add one letter to CUMIN DANCE and rearrange the rest to find a connection.

★★ Sunny Weather

Where will the sun shine knowing that each arrow points in the direction of a spot where the symbol is located? The symbols cannot be next to each other vertically, horizontally or diagonally. A symbol cannot be placed on top of an arrow. We show one symbol.

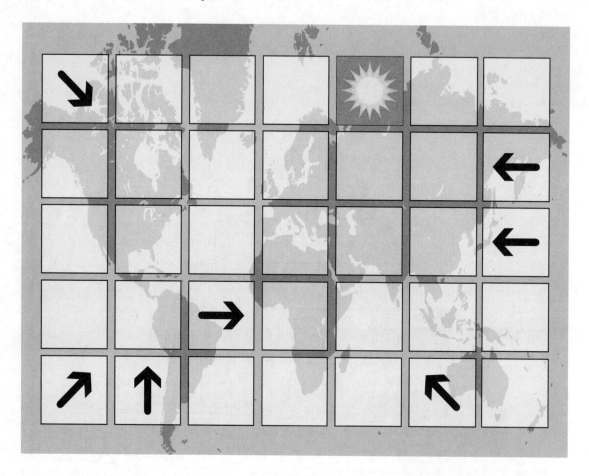

BLOCK ANAGRAM

Form the word that is described in the brackets with the letters above the grid. Extra letters are already in the right place.

TEA DRESS (hostess)

| S | | | W | | | | | |

★★★★ Case Crackers by John McCarthy

ACROSS

1 Narcissus spurned her
5 Palmer in *Moll Flanders*
10 Asset at Squaw Valley
14 Action-painting technique
15 *Gone With the Wind* actress Barbara
16 Tibetan monk
17 John Dickson Carr sleuth
19 Adam's grandson
20 Explorer Vespucci
21 Jean-Claude Van Damme film
23 Second vendition
24 Jimmy Carter's alma mater
25 Graceful seabird
27 Cause of yawning
30 More competent
33 *American Psycho* author
35 Sara of *Eastwick*
36 Where grass roots
37 Adduced
38 Waistcoat
39 Vichy water
40 Cargo bays
41 Mature efts
42 Catholicon
44 Aim at the barcode
46 Bittersweet covering
47 Orator
51 West Indies resorts
54 Bullish
55 Son of Ares
56 Erle Stanley Gardner sleuth
58 Aswan Dam locale
59 Japanese electronics company
60 A big person may come down with it
61 Ashe Stadium units
62 Joel Coen's brother
63 Auricles

DOWN

1 Mystery writer's award
2 Part of *CSI*
3 Animal skins
4 Runs
5 More protracted
6 The lowdown
7 Marvin in *The Dirty Dozen*
8 Air
9 Crystal Lake locale
10 45 cover
11 Carolyn Keene sleuth
12 *Typee* continuation
13 Narrow-waisted insect
18 Edmonton skater
22 Olympus Mons locale
26 *District 9* director Blomkamp
27 "God ___ America"
28 Remove from office
29 Citi Field nine
30 Baldwin in *The Aviator*
31 Boyfriend
32 *Remington Steele* sleuth
34 Inc. relative
37 Blow a big lead
38 Idolize
40 *License to Drive* star Corey
41 A Minor Prophet
43 Strikes out
45 Binney & Smith colorer
48 Campbell of *Martin*
49 "___ Own" (Bobby Brown hit)
50 Divides
51 Blue and Cross
52 "Acoustic Soul" singer India.___
53 Bench
54 "___ Little Tenderness"
57 Abbr. after Sen. Ayotte's name

★ Sudoku Twin

Fill in the grid so that each row, each column and each 3 x 3 frame contains every number from 1 to 9. A sudoku twin is two connected 9 x 9 sudokus.

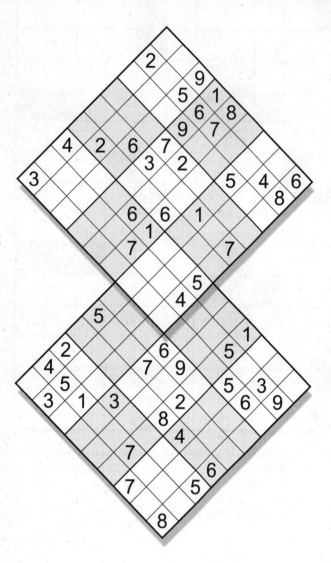

MISSING LETTER PROVERB

Fill in each missing letter, indicated by an X, to make a well-known proverb.

XAMXLIXRXTY XREXDX XONTXMPT

★ Cage the Animals

Draw lines to completely divide up the grid into small squares with exactly one animal per square. The squares should not overlap.

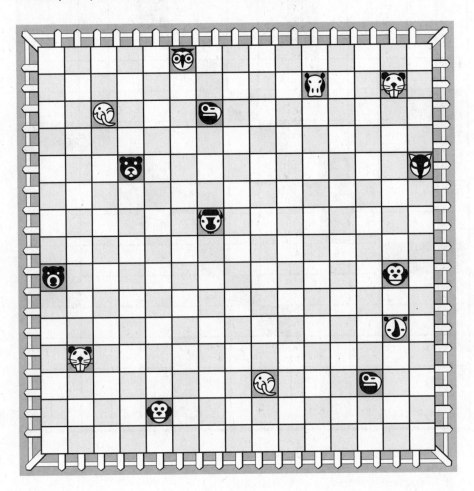

END GAME

The words you are seeking all have the letters END in them in the position indicated.
When you have found all of the answers, from the clues on the right, one column will reveal the END GAME word which is not so easy.

_	_	_	_	E	N	D	_	A Spanish house or estate
_	_	_	E	N	D	_	_	Additional material
_	_	_	_	E	N	D		A clergyman
_	_	_	E	N	D	_	_	Relied

★★★★ Themeless by Cindy Wheeler

ACROSS

1 Band of schemers
6 1600 on these is perfect
10 *The Thin Man* dog
14 *13 Days to Glory* subject
15 Persia now
16 "Want ___ a secret?"
17 Contract conditions
18 Delight
20 *Mission: Impossible* goal, at times
22 Pack animals
23 Cronelike
24 Nickname of Ernie Els
25 *Battle Cry* soldier
27 Majorino and Fey
28 *The Magic Flute* solo
29 Adhere
31 Beyond self-confident
35 The drink
36 Easter symbol
37 Dockworker's org.
38 Gets the bronze?
40 Lake near Reno
42 Glitch
43 Moiré-pattern painting
45 Mother ___
47 Peter in *Being There*
50 Ticket word
51 Hedge shrub
52 Like rotary phones
55 Strictly speaking
57 Fudd or Gantry
58 *Ace of Cakes* tool
59 Lofgren of the E Street Band
60 Bedtime story threesome
61 Hands on deck
62 Hydrotherapy havens
63 Palmer or Becker

DOWN

1 Old Deuteronomy's musical
2 Epithet of Athena
3 Conan, for one
4 Cleaning agent
5 ___ *Yonkers* (1993)
6 Prolonged attack
7 *Alfred* composer
8 Atlantic City's ___ Mahal
9 Coming down in flakes
10 Lacking purpose
11 1983 Indy winner Tom
12 Color wheel display
13 All atwitter
19 "Salute to the sun" discipline
21 Clunes in *Richard III*
24 Dog of song
25 Tall spar
26 Province
27 A size too small
30 Private jets
32 Redcoat's foe
33 Ending for cell
34 Green plum
39 Puzzle people
40 Highland plaids
41 Terminates
42 Ben in *Meet the Fockers*
44 Equal
46 Pond protozoan
47 ___-pea soup
48 *All My Children* vixen
49 .26 gallon
50 Bottomless pit
52 Clay pot
53 Bond girl Hatcher
54 Killarney language
56 It may be glossed over

★★★ BrainSnack®—Fingerprints

Which piece (1-6) should replace the question mark?

DOODLE PUZZLE

A doodle puzzle is a combination of images, letters and/or numbers that represent a word or a concept. If you cannot solve a doodle puzzle, do not look at the answer right away. Think hard—and outside the box.

OTHER 1

★ The Spy Who Came in From the Cold

The Puzzled Librarian was so busy fixing THE GOOD READS notice board, that she didn't see the stranger hovering beside the old card index files. The stranger pulled up a chair in front of them and took a piece of microfilm from his pocket and peered at it, holding it up to the light, then started to re-arrange the labels on the card index drawers. There is a message to be decoded. These numbers were on the microfilm:

13, 16, 24, 17, 19, 15, 7, 3, 29, 8, 23, 20, 14, 30, 28, 12, 21, 9, 26, 11, 5, 18, 25, 22, 6

LETTER LINE

Put a letter in each of the squares below to make a word which means "disclosure." These numbered clues refer to other words which can be made from the whole.

1 2 5 6 7 8 3 2 RELEVANT; 2 5 2 3 6 7 9 1 LIFT;
1 8 9 7 DISTURBANCE; 1 2 7 6 8 10 KEEP.

1	2	3	4	5	6	7	8	9	10

★★★★ On the Beach by Sam Bellotto Jr.

ACROSS

1 PD broadcast
4 Deep purple
8 Mollusk associated with clue* answers
12 Extinct ostrich cousin
13 Milo in *Ulysses*
15 Burgundy river
16 Species
17 Paying*
19 Pesky critter, informally
21 Noncommittal words
22 *To Kill a Mockingbird* author Lee
23 2009 Dillinger portrayer
24 River of Wales
27 Richard Branson's title
28 SpongeBob's home
30 Joke around
32 "America's Puppet Master"
34 Walk off with
35 Father of Cainan
37 Sound judgment
39 Buzz Lightyear's owner
40 "With tears of innocency and terms ___": Shak.
42 Toyota sedan
44 Narcotics agcy.
45 London calamity of 1666
47 Code-breaking org.
49 Skywalker's friend
50 Eyes of a poet
51 Rung
54 General concept
55 Marine gastropods
56 Dummy*
60 Happening last mo.
61 Mark's successors
62 One of Homer's sisters-in-law
63 Highland turndown
64 *Armageddon* author Uris
65 Green veggies
66 Affront, to Ice-T

DOWN

1 *Witness* cast
2 Mazurka's kin
3 Thirteen rolls*
4 Lithographic works
5 Poe house
6 "Just Like Jesse James" singer
7 Spitchcock ingredient
8 Crafty
9 Card game with forfeits
10 Babylonian god
11 Yogi Berra, in 1973
14 Visitor to Earth
15 Threaten a bite
18 Discredit a witness
20 Fol ___ cheese
23 They work the graveyard shift?
24 No longer bedridden*
25 Glissade
26 Tanzania neighbor
28 Golf instructor
29 Book-sale gp.
30 Retirement plan name
31 Prefix for structure
33 ___ and clear (no strings attached)
36 Red or Dead
38 Motel freebie
41 Not seeing eye to eye
43 Turning Stone Casino tribe
46 Bridge supports
48 York or Pepper: Abbr.
51 TV genre
52 Former Chinese premier Chou
53 Statesman Kefauver
54 Bettor's boast
55 Prompt beginning
56 *Snow White* frame
57 Tint
58 El Dorado treasure
59 With it

★★ Keep Going

Start on a blank square of your choice and connect as many blank squares as possible with one single continuous line. You can only connect squares along vertical and horizontal lines, not along diagonal lines. You must continue the connecting line up until the next obstacle, i.e. the rim of the box, a black square or a square that has already been used. You can change direction at any obstacle you meet. Each square can only be used once. The number of blank squares that will be left unused is marked in the upper square. There is more than one solution. We only show one solution.

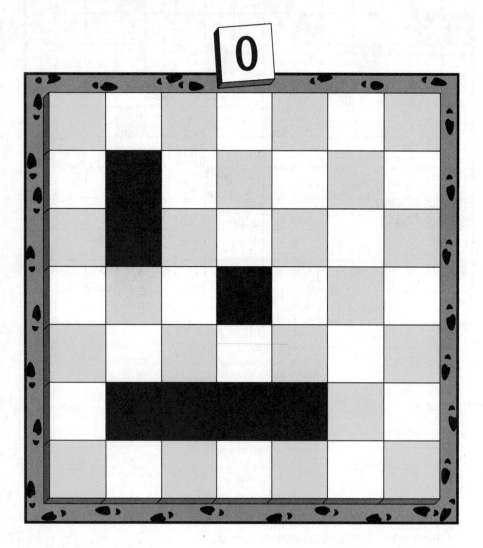

DELETE ONE

Delete one letter from **ON PAST INCOMES** and rearrange the rest to find a basis for reimbursement.

★ Health

All the words are hidden vertically, horizontally or diagonally—in both directions. The letters that remain unused form a sentence from left to right.

```
H E A L T H I S S A S T A T E
S U R G E R Y U E C H W O M B
A R O T C O D Y L I M A F R A
D E M E N T I A G F A T C T E
I C Q R I Y Z E N Y I S D B Y
A Z U T C C O M I R M I P L C
R E A S E N T T H E E G E H S
R M C I P A R I S T K O O E E
H A K T I N A N H R U L Y P L
E S E N I G C F C A E O A Y S
A L R E M E H E E R L R N T A
T E Y D A R E C A L A U A D E
H N D S S P A T A O S E O O M
P N E U M O N I A N P N X O C
C H R O M O S O M E I I Y L A
L I V A C C I N E W R T G B E
V L P R O S T H E S I S E F A
E N I L A N E R D A N R N R E
```

DEMENTIA
DENTIST
DIARRHEA
ECZEMA
FAMILY DOCTOR
FLU
HERNIA
INFECTION
LEUKEMIA
MEASLES
NEUROLOGIST
OXYGEN
PNEUMONIA
PREGNANCY
PROSTHESIS
QUACKERY
RETINA
SHINGLES
SURGERY
TRACHEA
VACCINE
VIRUS
WOMB

ADRENALINE
ARTERY

ASPIRIN
BLOOD TYPE

CHOLERA
CHROMOSOME

ONE LETTER LESS OR MORE

The word on the right side contains the letters of the word on the left side plus or minus the letter in the middle. One letter is already in the right place.

C H A R I S M A +R ☐ R ☐ ☐ ☐ ☐ ☐ ☐

★★★★ Expos I by Michele Sayer

ACROSS

1 Partner of Rinehart and Winston
5 "The Sweetheart of ___ -Chi"
10 Husband of Osiris
14 2,700-mile-long Asian river
15 Legal excuse
16 Ancient capital of Japan
17 ___ avis (nonpareil)
18 Stogie
19 Allowance after tare
20 Expo 2010 city
22 "Aw, c'mon!"
24 Bumpkin
25 Adhered
26 *The A-Team* actor
27 Sudan capital
30 Virginia Tech athlete
33 "Rebel Rouser" guitarist Eddy
34 123-45-6789 org.
35 "___ She Lovely": Wonder
36 Prove false
37 Industrial giant
38 The One, in *The Matrix*
39 Pixyish
40 Bar brew
41 Collegian's purchase
43 "The Bells" poet
44 "Jesus wept." is one
45 *Frasier* star
49 African chargers
51 Expo 88 city
52 A daughter of Eurytus
53 Splashdown site
55 Aerial maneuver
56 Birds and snakes do it
57 "I ___ what I said"
58 *Fools' Harvest* author Cox
59 *Rise of the Planet of the ___* (2011)
60 Alphabetizes
61 Timely face

DOWN

1 Spartan
2 Nebraska metropolis
3 Blue Ridge caverns
4 Convey
5 Scented bag
6 24-book epic
7 "I Remember it Well" musical
8 Wharton School degree
9 Wright bros. invention
10 Absorbed
11 Expo 2008 city
12 Angers
13 Appease
21 Richard in *Chicago*
23 A fly is a common one
25 Crochet stitch
27 Skating star Ilia
28 MQ-1 Predator org.
29 Trade center
30 Word to the wise
31 Hosea, in the Douay Bible
32 1982 World's Fair city
33 *Captain Singleton* author
36 Comes into one's own
37 Shivered
39 470-mile Spanish river
40 "___ I say, not ..."
42 Articles of faith
43 Publishes
45 18th U.S. president
46 Native New Zealander
47 Cookbook author Prudhomme
48 Fight off
49 *Green Mansions* girl
50 Croquet wicket
51 Grizzly
54 Major suit?

★★★ Sport Maze

Draw the shortest way from the ball to the goal. You can only move along vertical and horizontal lines, not along diagonal lines. The figure on each square indicates the number of squares the ball must be moved in the same direction. You can change direction at each stop.

4	5	1	5	5	2
1	4	4	1	2	5
2	1	2	3	4	4
3	4	2	●	0	3
5	4	4	3	1	5
3	1	3	1	3	1

UNCANNY TURN

Rearrange the letters of the phrase to form a cognate anagram, one which is related or connected in meaning to the original phrase. The answer can be one or more words.

NINE THUMPS

★★★★ Expos II by Michele Sayer

ACROSS

1 Adjudge
5 Base of a mesa
10 470-mile Spanish river
14 Designer Gernreich
15 "Horrible" Viking
16 Tenterhook
17 Half brother of Hermes
18 Ready to explode
19 A voided escutcheon
20 Expo 67 city
22 Béarnaise et al.
24 1946 Triple Crown horse
25 Midriff ___
26 Young goat
27 Brochure
30 Acknowledged expert
33 Gives a hoot
34 ABBA drummer Brunkert
35 "___ corny as Kansas ..."
36 Accepts a challenge
37 Sheepshank, e.g.
38 K—O links
39 Bad smelling
40 Goddess of the hunt
41 Greek philosopher
43 Sweetie pie
44 "Drat!" and "Egad!"
45 It's screened at JFK
49 Alien transport
51 Expo 58 city
52 *Christ Stopped at Eboli* author
53 Paddy in *Patriot Games*
55 Harness gait
56 Quarter
57 Family-tree apple
58 Aisne's end
59 Nirvana's "About a ___"
60 Abated
61 Mysterious loch

DOWN

1 Kind of queen
2 100-cent coins
3 "Lest we lose our ___": Browning
4 Boo-boos
5 Captain America's weapon
6 Tiffany weight
7 "___ in Calico" (Crosby hit)
8 Bandicoot
9 Makes conjectures
10 "All right already!"
11 Expo 1929 city
12 Incense
13 Hispanic hurrahs
21 Wreck
23 Heidi's home
25 Disrobed
27 Expo 1937 city
28 PayPal founder Musk
29 Car company of India
30 .001-inch units
31 A few rounds, perhaps
32 Expo 86 city
33 *Drop Dead Fred* actress Phoebe
36 Leave without power?
37 Trio who sang "Greenback Dollar"
39 The inevitable
40 "Mad ___ and Englishmen": Coward
42 Ethnic
43 Transported
45 Fanny in *Funny Girl*
46 John Denver album
47 Lipstick type
48 *Blue Bloods* actor Will
49 Bessemer leftover
50 Air: Comb. form
51 Honey bunch
54 Long in *Big Momma's House 2*

★ Spot the Differences

Find the nine differences in the image on the right.

CHANGE ONE

Change one letter in each of these two words to form a common two-word phrase.

SHOOTING CATCH

★★★ Sudoku

Fill in the grid so that each row, each column and each 3 x 3 frame contains every number from 1 to 9.

						1		
4							2	
							6	4
	1				2			
	2	8		7	4			
9	7	6		5				
		1		4	7			9
		9		8	5			1
				1		7		2

SQUIRCLES

Place consonants in the squares and vowels in the circles and form words in each vertical column. The definitions of the words you are looking for are listed. (The grid will reveal the names of two sports.)

1 Made in advance
2 A republic in Africa
3 From side to side
4 Fight
5 Loud confused noise
6 Large fleet
7 A showy ornament, trinket or article of clothing
8 A hydrocarbon radical

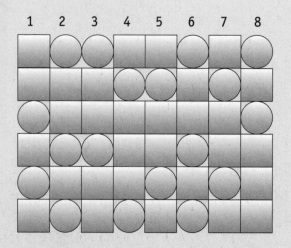

★★★ Word Sudoku

Complete the grid so that each row, each column and each 3 x 3 frame contains the nine letters from the black box below. The hidden nine-letter word is in the diagonal from top left to bottom right.

A M N O P R S T X

	A			P		R	O	T
		R						
X					M			
	O		R		A	T		
	S	P						
	N		A	S	P			
			N				O	
				N			X	

DOODLE PUZZLE

A doodle puzzle is a combination of images, letters and/or numbers that represent a word or a concept. If you cannot solve a doodle puzzle, do not look at the answer right away. Think hard—and outside the box.

noon Mid

★★★ BrainSnack®—Cubism

Which group of cubes (1-5) does not belong?

UNCANNY TURN

Rearrange the letters of the phrase to form a cognate anagram, one which is related or connected in meaning to the original phrase. The answer can be one or more words.

HAD INDIAN RIG

★★★★ College Teams I by Don Law

ACROSS

1 Dearth
5 Running wild
9 Hoopster
14 Asian range
15 Spreadsheet filler
16 Reference marks
17 Big Green of the Ivy League
19 Lasso loop
20 Slope downward
21 Winning roll of 7
23 Yokohama "yes"
24 Percussion instrument
25 A gear
29 Most easily heard
32 De la Garza of *Law & Order*
33 "Oh My My" singer Ringo
35 High crest
36 Scuba gear
37 Entrance courts
38 Wry grimace
39 *Dracula* director Browning
40 Wintry precip
41 Be a water witch
42 Aseptic
44 Actress De Carlo and others
46 Drumhead company
47 EMT destinations
48 Lucky ___ foot
51 PEN members
55 Bearded sheep
56 Tigers of the Ivy League
58 Nile mouth
59 Gaels of the MAAC
60 Wolf who adopted Mowgli
61 Acetate, for one
62 Cat's-paw
63 Challenge to a duel

DOWN

1 *This Gun for Hire* actor Alan
2 Mercury's wings
3 2006 Pixar film
4 Appliance centers?
5 Handsome fellow
6 Adams in *Octopussy*
7 Hall-of-Fame Giant
8 "It Had to Be You" lyricist
9 Profile
10 Teem
11 Hoyas of the Big East
12 *Born Free* beast
13 Cambodian moolah
18 Anne in *Reality Bites*
22 Where Socrates shopped
25 White-water craft
26 Creator of J. Alfred Prufrock
27 Commodores of the SEC
28 First name in cosmetics
29 Flock
30 Boozehound
31 Shady street liners
34 A quarter of dodici
37 Deal out
38 ___ vs. Aliens (2009)
40 Much the same
41 Greek column style
43 Payback
45 March equinox
48 Brusque
49 *Xena: Warrior Princess* villain
50 Skewer
51 A.A. candidate
52 Latin for "and others"
53 Downey in *A Woman Named Jackie*
54 Cinch
57 One of Pooh's pals

★ Cage the Animals

Draw lines to completely divide up the grid into small squares with exactly one animal per square. The squares should not overlap.

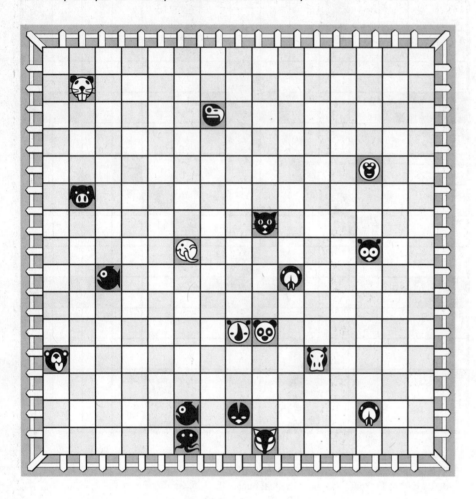

FRIENDS

What do the following words have in common?

BORE DUKE FREE KING OFFICIAL RAN STAR

★★ Binairo

Complete the grid with zeros and ones until there are 5 zeros and 6 ones in every row and every column. No more than two of the same number can be next to or under each other. Rows or columns with exactly the same content are not allowed. There is only one valid solution.

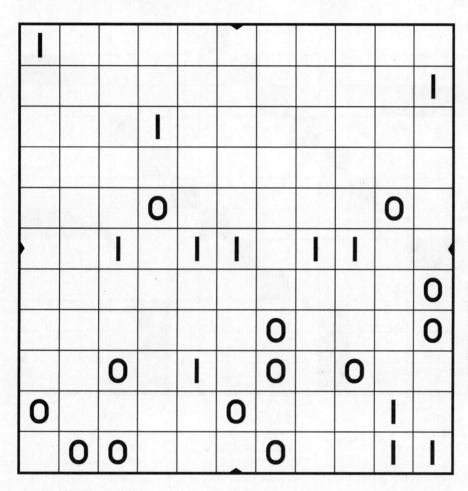

SANDWICH

What four-letter word belongs between the word at left and the word at right, so that the first and second word, and the second and third word, each form a common compound word or phrase?

THUMB _ _ _ _ BRUSH

★★★★ College Teams II by Don Law

ACROSS

1 *The Lion King* baddie
5 "Goodbye, Gabrielle"
10 Center the pigskin
14 Silent film star Negri
15 Burger topper
16 Gdansk resident
17 Dead set against
18 Saints of the MAAC
19 To ___ (exactly)
20 Cardinal of the Pac-12
22 Miguel in *Traffic*
24 Messenger of the gods
25 Minotaur's home
26 Spheroid
27 Pantomime game
30 View from Everest
33 Salk's conquest
34 Arabic name
35 "Make It Funky" rapper
36 Natural disaster
37 Persian Gulf country
38 As needed: Rx
39 Pontifical cape
40 Dignified manners
41 Solar phenomena
43 Fed Chairman Bernanke
44 ___ *Evil* (Mia Farrow film)
45 Kind of map
49 Afloat
51 Lions of the Ivy League
52 "As ___ going to St. Ives ..."
53 2011 hurricane
55 Word in a counting-out rhyme
56 Jared in *Fight Club*
57 Conger catcher
58 Anders Fogh Rasmussen's org.
59 Tree of Knowledge setting
60 *Midnight Cowboy* con man
61 Larger ___ life

DOWN

1 Charley horse, e.g.
2 Medieval fable
3 Site for some rites
4 Columbo's trademark
5 Take up, in a way
6 Jersey farm
7 Chilled
8 Huge time frame
9 Not likely to quail
10 Achaean League member
11 Fighting Irish of the Big East
12 Marine heading
13 Look intently
21 Secure Old Glory
23 Saarinen of architecture
25 Agnew of Celtic Woman
27 Lets the A/C run
28 Dashing style
29 Seven are deadly
30 Bites lightly
31 Curtain color
32 Nittany Lions of the Big Ten
33 Student of Socrates
36 "The Last ___" (Alaska nickname)
37 Salve
39 Aboveboard's partner
40 Pop-up list
42 162 MLB games, e.g.
43 Ravel's most famous work
45 Traffic markers
46 Jamaican witchcraft
47 Utah range
48 Synthetic fabric
49 It flows for 4,180 miles
50 In amazement
51 Prehistoric ax
54 Stephen of *Princess Caraboo*

★ Astronomy

All the words are hidden vertically, horizontally or diagonally—in both directions. The letters that remain unused form a sentence from left to right.

```
G A L I L E O B I G B A N G A
J U P I T E R Z O D I A C S T
R O N O Y S P V N E P T U N E
M Y Y I R R S L E L B B U H O
M A R S U E Y S U N A R U E N
E W O F C V R S A T U R N L T
H Y P E R I O N H E O S F I E
A K O W E N T C O M E T L O S
W L L C M U A E I R E E E C T
K I A N C E V N S O I K V E E
I M R N W O R T H E I C A N L
N C I H L A E A R T H O R T E
G M S L A T S U E E U R T R S
P H O T O N B R R M S C E I C
A P N P L A O X Y G E N C S O
A N D R O M E D A N A S A M P
Y T I V A R G Y A N A C P T E
I V E R E A L U B E N O S L E
```

GALILEO
GRAVITY
HAWKING
HELIOCENTRISM
HUBBLE
HYPERION
JUPITER
MARS
MERCURY
METEOR
MILKY WAY
NASA
NEBULAE
NEPTUNE
OBSERVATORY
OXYGEN
PHOTON
PLUTO
POLARIS
ROCKET
SATURN
SPACE TRAVEL
TELESCOPE
UNIVERSE
URANUS
VENUS
ZODIAC

ANDROMEDA
APOLLO

BIG BANG
CENTAUR

COMET
EARTH

LETTERBLOCKS

Move the letterblocks around so that words are formed on top and below that you can associate with countries.

★★ Keep Going

Start on a blank square of your choice and connect as many blank squares as possible with one single continuous line. You can only connect squares along vertical and horizontal lines, not along diagonal lines. You must continue the connecting line up until the next obstacle, i.e. the rim of the box, a black square or a square that has already been used. You can change direction at any obstacle you meet. Each square can only be used once. The number of blank squares that will be left unused is marked in the upper square. There is more than one solution. We only show one solution.

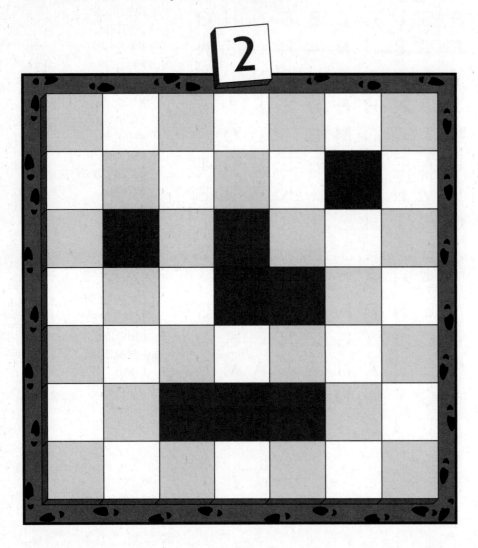

REPOSITION PREPOSITION

Unscramble TITAN DOWN THINGS and find a one-word preposition.

★★★★ Themeless by Karen Peterson

ACROSS

1 61 subject
6 Minor to-do
10 Talk trash
14 Like Crusoe before Friday
15 RPM instrument
16 Cut glass
17 Blooming early
18 Meddle
20 A, B, and C
22 Became itinerant
23 Cream of the crop
24 Picture puzzles
25 "Cowboy's Lament" city
27 Steen's stand
28 Tony Romo targets
29 Aida's native land
31 Shell food?
35 *Bleak House* girl
36 16-oz. units
37 *Dracula* director Browning
38 "Amazing Grace," e.g.
40 Struck a low blow
42 Golfer Irwin
43 Tale of Troy
45 Adds a rider to
47 Bawdy
50 "Dear" book
51 *Guys and Dolls* gambler Detroit
52 Like chronicles of the past
55 False
57 Beehive-shaped crown
58 Bittersweet coating
59 ___ *plaisir!*
60 Step onstage
61 Bucolic expanses
62 Acuff and Clark
63 About one-ninth of an orchestra

DOWN

1 "Terrif!"
2 Kirghizian range
3 Netherlands city
4 Inspires
5 Apparently was
6 Service hitch
7 *Iron Chef* props
8 Play God?
9 *Black Widow* actress Russell
10 A fate worse than debt
11 Romantic pairs
12 Hillside debris
13 Backyard buildings
19 Housecoat
21 Religious painting
24 Striker's demand
25 "Ah!___!" (Donnie Iris song)
26 Murray of tennis
27 Abated
30 Arm bones
32 "Be that as it may ..."
33 Like vichyssoise
34 Pablo Neruda poems
39 *The Graduate* director
40 *As Good as It Gets* actor Greg
41 Place for a speaker
42 Anne of Green Gables, e.g.
44 Low-fat
46 Substance
47 Shaq of basketball
48 Fonteyn's rail
49 Anatomical furrow
50 Harrow blades
52 "Hip to Be Square" rocker Lewis
53 All het up
54 "Drive" band
56 Ab ___ (from the beginning)

★★★ Sport Maze

Draw the shortest way from the ball to the goal. You can only move along vertical and horizontal lines, not along diagonal lines. The figure on each square indicates the number of squares the ball must be moved in the same direction. You can change direction at each stop.

(ball)	5	5	5	2	1 (goal)
2	3	1	4	2	1
3	3	0	3	3	2
4	2	3	2	2	5
4	2	4	1	2	1
1	2	1	2	1	2

DOUBLETALK

What word means "to adhere" or "a piece of wood"?

★★★ Kakuro

Each number in a black area is the sum of the numbers that you have to enter in the next empty boxes. The empty boxes that make up the sum are called a run. The sum of the across run is written above the diagonal in the black area and the sum of the down run is written below the diagonal. Runs can only contain the numbers 1 through 9 and each number in a run can only be used once. The gray boxes only contain odd numbers and the white only even numbers.

TRANSADDITION

Add one letter to LENT RACE ID and rearrange the rest to find a connection.

★★★★ Themeless by Karen Peterson

ACROSS

1 Sudden contraction
6 Long-neck pear
10 A flat, thick piece
14 " ___ la vista, baby"
15 Odd, in Orkney
16 "All I Want ___": Sugarland
17 *Bordertown* star
20 Starring roles
21 *Good Guys Wear Black* actor Chuck
22 Cast an amorous eye
23 Sean in *Medicine Man*
24 Be pleasing (to)
26 Swahili's language group
27 Those born on July 31
28 Autocrats of yore
30 Egg-salad ingredient
34 *Apollo 13* lifeboat
35 *Boyz n the Hood* role
36 Dixie soldier
37 Ditto, in footnotes
39 Tom's *Splash* costar
41 Edvard Munch Museum site
42 Hilltop home
44 San Marino locale
46 Apparition
49 "Nights in White ___": Moody Blues
50 Agenda item
51 Diametric
54 Food grinder?
56 River of central Germany
57 First name in daredevilry
58 Prefix for mural
59 Jockeyed
60 Mark of approval
61 Resource

DOWN

1 1979 Iranian exile
2 Postal sheet
3 First enclosed stadium
4 Stoolies
5 Brown paper
6 Got on the ump
7 Ghostly forms
8 Toledo Mrs.
9 Mortars
10 Breastbone
11 Peter in *Beat the Devil*
12 *Surfing the Zeitgeist* novelist
13 Holstein handle
18 Like helium
19 "___ Worry, Be Happy"
23 "Can't Let Go" singer Mariah
24 Giantess who wrestled Thor
25 "A friend in ___ ..."
26 Balanchine's beam
29 *The Winding ___* (1925)
31 Lawless lighters
32 Online consumer guide
33 Clarinet cousin
38 Like Stephen King's oeuvre
39 Deepens a waterway
40 Abrupt transitions
41 Devout petitions
43 Sicily's highest peak
45 Shangri-la
46 "Night Moves" singer Bob
47 Madrid museum
48 Acted human
49 "Tell me the details!"
51 Athenian theaters
52 Weight without cargo
53 Israeli resort city
55 Vigil

★★★ BrainSnack®—Painter

Which paint (1-4) was used the most to color in the three shapes?

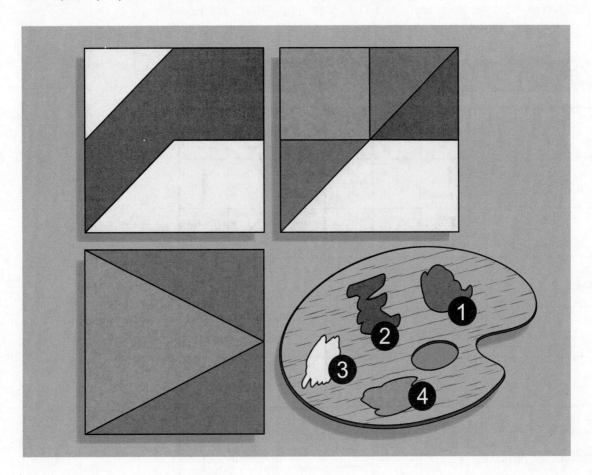

BLOCK ANAGRAM

Form the words that are described in the brackets with the letters above the grid. Extra letters are already in the right place.

NORDIC ALP (major part of the central nervous system)

| S | | | | | | | | | | | |

★★★ Word Sudoku

Complete the grid so that each row, each column and each 3 x 3 frame contains the nine letters from the black box below. The hidden nine-letter word is in the diagonal from top left to bottom right.

A B D E I L R T V

	A	B	I		V		D	E
			L					I
L		B						
A		I						
	E			I		D	V	
D		V						
	D							T
				L	T	I		A

MISSING LETTER PROVERB

Fill in each missing letter, indicated by an X, to make a well-known proverb.

XILENXE IX XOLXEN

★★★ BrainSnack®—Number Block

Which number should replace the question mark?

END GAME

The words you are seeking all have the letters END in them in the position indicated.
When you have found all of the answers, from the clues on the right, one column will reveal the
END GAME word which radiates.

_	_	_	_	E	N	D	_	_	Riser
_	_	_	_	E	N	D	_	_	Straightened
_	_	_	E	N	D	_	_		Repaired again
_	_	E	N	D	_	_	_		Much improving

★★★★ Doctor Who by Sam Bellotto Jr.

ACROSS

1 "Spark" singer Tori
5 Three-horse open sleigh
11 Item in an ICU
14 Marsh bird
15 King of Morocco (1961–1999)
16 Merkel in *The Mad Doctor of Market Street*
17 Dr. Mark Craig's hospital, familiarly
19 Country legend Acuff
20 Ultra-ultra
21 Miami Heat home
22 "My Way" lyricist
23 Dog food brand
25 Takes the lead?
27 Mary Shelley's doctor
31 Hospital staffer
32 Slimy stuff
33 Over half of Israel
37 Balin in *The Young Doctors*
38 *ER* wardrobe item
41 Mystifier Geller
42 Rival of Paris
44 Sunflower state: Abbr.
45 Champions Tour members
46 Misanthropic TV doctor
50 Lettuce variety
53 It's found in bars
54 "Alphabet Song" start
55 Saying
57 Southern Cal mascot
61 Push-up muscle
62 Russian doctor of fiction
64 Bar opening?
65 Crème ___
66 Eternally
67 She played Dr. Breene on *Third Watch*
68 Founder of modern astronomy
69 ___ avis

DOWN

1 Adjutant: Abbr.
2 Sleuth played by Lorre
3 "Milk's favorite cookie"
4 Soup cracker
5 "I am the Alpha and ___": Rev. 1:8
6 Like sushi tuna
7 Dept. of Labor arm
8 "Oh, East ___, and West is West ..."
9 Tae kwon do's kin
10 Suffix for prop
11 *M*A*S*H* doctor
12 Gourmet mushroom
13 Rabbinic judge
18 Prepare beans
22 Obama cabineteer Duncan
24 Elitist
26 "Is so!" rebuttal
27 Inside the foul line
28 Left-leaning GOPer
29 Dr. Bricker on *The Love Boat*
30 "Boffo!"
34 Mentor
35 Psyche's lover
36 Workshop tool
38 Petty in *Free Willy*
39 Eight in a row?
40 "A rose by ___ name ...": Shak.
43 Falstaffian oath
45 Hollow roll
47 Safeguard
48 Get ready
49 Mata of espionage
50 Lickety-split
51 Like Mrs. Spratt
52 Capt. Kirk's doctor
56 "The doctor ___ see you now"
58 Starbucks quaff
59 Antiquing device
60 Ibsen's Helmer
62 H.S. publication
63 Zorro's mark

★★ Sudoku X

Fill in the grid so that each row, each column and each 3 x 3 frame contains every number from 1 to 9. The two main diagonals of the grid also contain every number from 1 to 9.

								2
					1	8		7
		8	4	2			3	1
7							5	8
			2		4	9		3
3		4		5	9			
8		1						
9			5	3			2	
				9	6	7		

UNCANNY TURN

Rearrange the letters of the phrase to form a cognate anagram, one which is related or connected in meaning to the original phrase. The answer can be one or more words.

DICK STRUMS

★ Cage the Animals

Draw lines to completely divide up the grid into small squares with exactly one animal per square. The squares should not overlap.

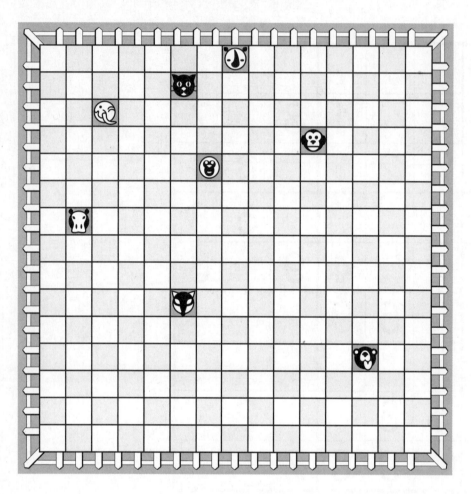

CHANGELINGS

Each of the three lines of letters below spell words which have an engineering connection, but the letters have been mixed up. Four letters from the first word are now in the third line, four letters from the third word are in the second line and four letters from the second word are in the first line. The remaining letters are in their original places. What are the words?

M O H O N O T I A E
O E C R A P I C W L
H L C S E M O V E R

★★★★★ Homophones by John M. Samson

ACROSS

1 Blacken on the grill
5 Set in concrete
10 IRS functionaries
14 Senator's staffer
15 Emmy winner Gibbons
16 Architect's plinth
17 Not moving
19 Bearing
20 A Barbary state
21 "___ makes the heart ..."
23 Hurling and curling
24 Army cadet org.
25 "Waiting for the Robert ___"
27 Chewing one's cud
30 Plains dwelling
33 'Hoods
35 Friend
36 Not theirs
37 Crack up
38 Half of MCIV
39 3-D medical scan
40 Mr. Magoo's nephew
41 Danse Macabre composer Saint-___
42 Clever remarks
44 Appear to be
46 Shoreline recess
47 Kathmandu native
51 Web crawlers
54 Adjusted to fit
55 "Absolutely not!"
56 Homophone of 17-Across
58 Humanoid race in Stargate SG-1
59 Airborne toys
60 Environmental science: Abbr.
61 Moolah
62 Dennis Miller's ___, Therefore I Am
63 Rostrum

DOWN

1 Fills roles
2 Approach for money
3 Hersey bell town
4 AARP makeup
5 Kay Thompson heroine
6 Suvari in American Beauty
7 "Billy, Don't ___ Hero"
8 Henry Aldrich star Stone
9 Cockcrow
10 Bill Haley's group
11 Fundamental truth
12 Guinness in The Horse's Mouth
13 40-decibel unit
18 Agave fiber
22 Mama's boys
26 Anglo-Saxon governors
27 Legendary cowboy Bill
28 "You're So ___": Simon
29 First Olympics site
30 Burial chamber
31 Continental coin
32 Homophone of 11-Down
34 Seabiscuit's jockey Pollard
37 Ride behind a boat
38 Hosed down
40 Made a tapestry
41 Be responsible for
43 Demure
45 Answer the call
48 Asian palm
49 ___ Soleil (Louis XIV)
50 Bucolic writings
51 Like a bug in a rug
52 Johnnycake
53 Mix it up
54 Sun god
57 ___ loss for words

★★ Keep Going

Start on a blank square of your choice and connect as many blank squares as possible with one single continuous line. You can only connect squares along vertical and horizontal lines, not along diagonal lines. You must continue the connecting line up until the next obstacle, i.e. the rim of the box, a black square or a square that has already been used. You can change direction at any obstacle you meet. Each square can only be used once. The number of blank squares that will be left unused is marked in the upper square. There is more than one solution. We only show one solution.

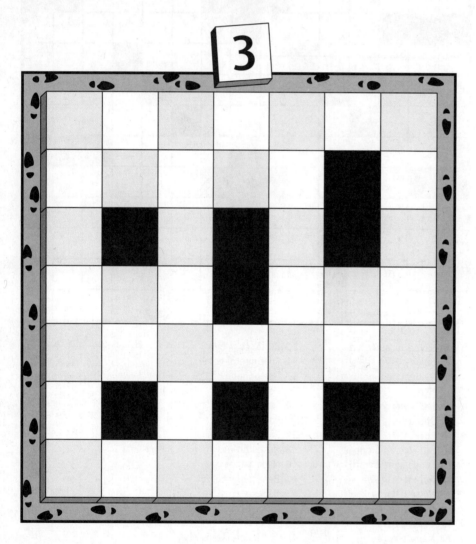

DELETE ONE

Delete one letter from FITS MANIACS and rearrange the rest to find an appropriate category.

★ Telecommunications

All the words are hidden vertically, horizontally or diagonally—in both directions. The letters that remain unused form a sentence from left to right.

```
I N L A C O L C O M P A N Y T
M H E P A S T I F Y S O U W A
B E A M O F L I G H T O E N T
E W S D T I O P L L H X U E I
K I O S N E D A S L P O L N M
A R E M A C N A E E O B T N D
E E O D T G H E R B A E Y E S
N L Y W I O E I U C R P V T P
R E L S T G M S E N S I E A E
S S E A D E I A E B C L G N A
C S U X N T N T T E I O A T K
N I T T E O O A A B T A M E E
T C R R A L Z C O L T N I N R
T H H T E S E M A T T A E N N
F A X A C T E T I O N L O A F
T H I N T E R N A T I O N A L
C H A N N E L E D S W G I T C
H B O A R D O E P E R A T O R
```

CAMERA
CHANNEL
CHAT
COMPANY
DEVICE
DIGITAL
ELECTRIC
EXPERIMENT
FAX
IMAGE
INTERNATIONAL
INTERNET
LOCAL
MESSAGES
MOBILE
NETWORK
RADIO
SEND
SIGNAL
SOUND
SPEAKER
TELEX
WIRELESS
ZONAL

ANALOG   BEAM OF LIGHT   BYTE
ANTENNA   BELL   CABLE

CHANGE ONE

Change one letter in each of these two words to form a common two-word phrase.

BOLD SWEAR

★★★★★ First Name Last by John M. Samson

ACROSS

1 Breakfast order
5 Alaskan salmon
9 Painter Durand
14 "Encore!"
15 La Scala solo
16 Impertinent
17 Po player in a casino game?
19 Carvel of 1492
20 Limited ___
21 "I Dood It" comedian
23 *Moll Flanders* author Defoe
24 *Earth in the Balance* subj.
25 Hispanic huzzahs
27 Contest forms
30 "FOR SALE," e.g.
33 Abided
35 Lose control
36 No-brainer card game
37 Bus. card address
38 Parched
39 "___ Around": Beach Boys
41 Face reddener
43 Highland girl
44 Foot jewelry
46 Gray-brown goose
48 Da ___, Vietnam
49 Sheepish reply?
53 Called on
56 Individuals
57 *Green Acres* cow
58 Floor a stand-up comedian?
60 "Be patient!"
61 "Chiquitita" band
62 Bay State motto word
63 White as a sheet
64 Lillian in *Birth of a Nation*
65 Active ingredient in Off!

DOWN

1 Assign journalists to military units
2 *A Woman Called ___* (1982)
3 Buckwheat, e.g.
4 Orange segment
5 Blandished
6 "Is it a hit ___ error?"
7 Barfly's two cents
8 Acorn droppers
9 Appearance
10 *H.M.S. Pinafore* extras
11 Stalk an *NCIS: Los Angeles* star?
12 "Outer" prefix
13 Reynolds in *Green Lantern*
18 Richard of *Jaws* fame
22 Clark of *Smallville*
26 Batted
27 "Bat Out of Hell" singer Foley
28 Trophy sides
29 1974 CIA-spoof movie
30 "Hot Lips" portrayer
31 Othello's lieutenant
32 Jealous *Rat Race* actor?
34 .0000001 joule
40 Apprentice
41 Cannes cherub
42 Wife of Isaac
43 Not able to run free
45 Resident doctor
47 "Popeye" Doyle, for one
50 Carried (by)
51 Absinthe flavor
52 Strong suit
53 *Home Again* host Bob
54 Cleopatra's maid
55 Mrs. Doubtfire's attire
56 Water pollutants
59 *Madama Butterfly* accessory

★★★ BrainSnack®—Energy Saver

The owners of this modern house are trying to limit energy use to a minimum.
Each number stands for the use in a certain room. How much energy will be
used in the room with the question mark (the main entrance)?

LETTER LINE

Put a letter in each of the squares below to make a word which means "inspiring fear." These
numbered clues refer to other words which can be made from the whole.

8 7 5 9 10 6 RELEASED ON BOND; 9 5 4 8 2 IN BETWEEN;
8 3 5 10 1 SHORT; 8 9 7 6 10 KNIFE; 8 10 6 9 7 4 CHAOS.

1	2	3	4	5	6	7	8	9	10

★★ Monkey Business

Some of the older students have been monkeying about with the BEST KIDS BOOKS titles list in the library. Can you fix it?

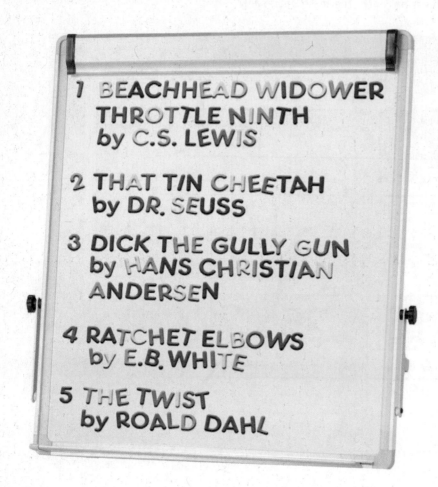

1 BEACHHEAD WIDOWER THROTTLE NINTH
by C.S. LEWIS

2 THAT TIN CHEETAH
by DR. SEUSS

3 DICK THE GULLY GUN
by HANS CHRISTIAN ANDERSEN

4 RATCHET ELBOWS
by E.B. WHITE

5 THE TWIST
by ROALD DAHL

ONE LETTER LESS OR MORE

The word on the right side contains the letters of the word on the left side plus or minus the letter in the middle. One letter is already in the right place.

L O C A T I O N +I □ □ □ **L** □ □ □ □

★★★★★ Last Name First by John M. Samson

ACROSS

1 Ice-cream preference
5 *Caveman* star Ringo
10 Hole makers
14 *Bolero* instrument
15 "... and baby makes ___"
16 Flight of steps to a riverbank
17 Impressionist who needs a lift?
19 Adjutant
20 Beguiled
21 A time to dye
23 Apply spin
24 Parson's place
25 Arizona plant
28 Mardi Gras
31 Called for liniment
32 Retrogressing
33 Citrus cooler
34 *Abbey* ___ album
35 Barely burn
36 Fannie Mae: Abbr.
37 "___ bodkins!"
38 Zellweger in *Bridget Jones's Diary*
39 Bamboo stems
40 Conferences
42 Supple
43 Ben in *Chariots of Fire*
44 Rapunzel's claim to fame
45 *Mutiny on the Bounty* island
47 Force upon again
51 Drummer Van Halen
52 Tan *Fringe* actress?
54 Tribe of Israel
55 *12 Angry Men* director
56 Starbuck's skipper
57 Stubby in "Cat Ballou"
58 "By jove!"
59 Big season at Toys "R" Us

DOWN

1 Keep back
2 Anne Nichols hero
3 Campus cadet org.
4 Abhorred
5 Allen and Martin
6 Chucked
7 Adjective for Death Valley
8 DVR button
9 Drill
10 1994 U.S. Open winner
11 Game show lady goes platinum blonde?
12 Do dock work
13 An end to fun?
18 Ariel Sharon's party
22 "Snowbird" singer Murray
24 One of the Simpsons
25 Rebound
26 Kipling's "___ of Morals"
27 Pursue a *Community* star?
28 Traffic markers
29 Blurb specialists
30 Rock-bottom
32 "Silly Love Songs" band
35 Displaying good judgment
36 What turnabout is
38 Street fight
39 "___ Ev'ry Mountain"
41 *Hi and Lois* baby
42 Spotted ponies
44 Chopped down
45 Blab
46 Epithet of Athena
47 Eternal City
48 *Hawaii Five-O* setting
49 Earth's crust
50 Kathryn of *Law & Order: CI*
53 Trapdoor cover

★★★ Sport Maze

Draw the shortest way from the ball to the goal. You can only move along vertical and horizontal lines, not along diagonal lines. The figure on each square indicates the number of squares the ball must be moved in the same direction. You can change direction at each stop.

1	4	5	4	2	5
5	2	3	2	3	3
1	4	2	1	4	1
5	4	3	1	3	5
2	1	4	3	2	3
3	1	4	1	●	3

UNCANNY TURN

Rearrange the letters of the phrase to form a cognate anagram, one which is related or connected in meaning to the original phrase. The answer can be one or more words.

MY MOM

★★★ Word Sudoku

Complete the grid so that each row, each column and each 3 x 3 frame contains the nine letters from the black box below. The hidden nine-letter word is in the diagonal from top left to bottom right.

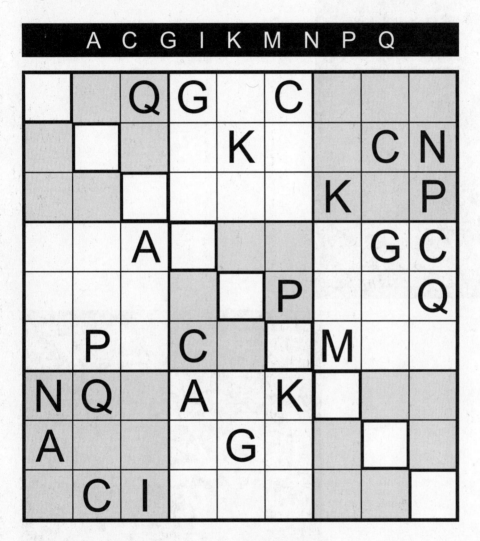

A C G I K M N P Q

	Q	G			C			
			K				C	N
					K			P
	A						G	C
				P				Q
P		C			M			
N	Q		A		K			
A			G					
	C	I						

DOODLE PUZZLE

A doodle puzzle is a combination of images, letters and/or numbers that represent a word or a concept. If you cannot solve a doodle puzzle, do not look at the answer right away. Think hard—and outside the box.

★ Spot the Differences

Find the nine differences in the image on the right.

DELETE ONE

Delete one letter from CURE OR SPIN and rearrange the rest to find the dealers.

★★★★★ Wines by John M. Samson

ACROSS

1 Borscht ingredient
5 Honey-colored
10 *Teacher's Pet* dog
14 Irish Gaelic
15 Witherspoon in *Water for Elephants*
16 Shroud
17 Masonry support
18 Kellogg's Pop-___
19 Novelist Bagnold
20 Flowery white wine
22 Leek relatives
24 Superlative Lake Tanganyika
25 With a good physique
26 Muesli morsel
27 Helena resident
30 Chief island of the Philippines
33 Nutritionist's topics
34 "Yang Yang" singer Yoko
35 PGA winner Dutra
36 Superhero wear
37 ___-Japanese War
38 Recyclable item
39 Opposite of hindered
40 Buckeye State city
41 In the know
43 LVII + XCIV
44 Nom de guerre
45 They'll curl your hair
49 Kindling
51 Sweet white wine
52 "Just You ___": Manchester
53 Newscast feature
55 FDR's dog
56 Home of Keebler elves
57 Egglike
58 School on the Rio Grande
59 Is under the weather
60 Of birth
61 Not so great

DOWN

1 Abe Lincoln grew one
2 Banks of baseball
3 Lauder of cosmetics
4 Cough syrup measure
5 Creative type
6 "And I said what I ___": Seuss
7 Composer of *Wozzeck*
8 Ottawa hrs.
9 Fills the air
10 Aussie girl
11 Full-bodied red wine
12 King of the Aesir
13 *Bill & ___ Excellent Adventure* (1989)
21 Rest against
23 Picky people pick 'em
25 Reacted to a bad call
27 Power bike
28 ___ Domini
29 Twelve sharp
30 Focal points
31 Polish lancer
32 Robust red wine
33 Grows ghostly
36 Oklahoma panhandle river
37 Virtuosic
39 Indy winner Luyendyk
40 Garfunkel's "___ Know"
42 Doo-wop selections
43 Coerce
45 *Giant* ranch
46 Put on cloud nine
47 Dramatis personae
48 Loses it
49 "See ya!"
50 Letters on the cross
51 Sing like Cleo Laine
54 Mendes in *Ghost Rider*

★★ Sudoku X

Fill in the grid so that each row, each column and each 3 x 3 frame contains every number from 1 to 9. The two main diagonals of the grid also contain every number from 1 to 9.

	2				8			
			4				5	
7								
			9	1				
8	3		6			2		
1				4				
		1				6	8	
	9		3		7			2
	6					7		4

FRIENDS

What do the following words have in common?

ACCIDENT CLERIC COMIC CRITIC LOGIC
NORM PERSON

★ Cage the Animals

Draw lines to completely divide up the grid into small squares with exactly one animal per square. The squares should not overlap.

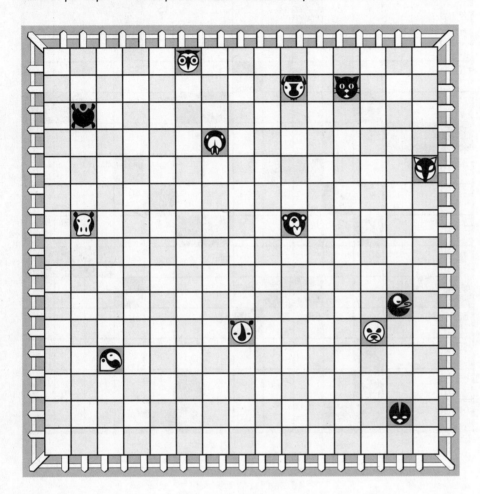

SANDWICH

What four-letter word belongs between the word at left and the word at right, so that the first and second word, and the second and third word, each form a common compound word or phrase?

COPPER _ _ _ _ HUNTER

★★★★★ Seafarers by Sam Bellotto Jr.

ACROSS

1 Hamburg's river
5 Tall Corn State
9 Faulty
12 December songs
14 Arctic goose
16 Ketel ___ vodka
17 *Ellen* actress
19 Put away
20 Suggested
21 Aran knitwear
23 "Wahoo!"
24 *24 Hours* novelist
26 Put the cuffs on
27 Man on the $10,000 bill
32 Conned
35 *Zuckerman Unbound* author
36 Pine flow
37 Lena of *Alias*
38 "You ___ see this!"
40 Missile or sneaker
41 Def in *Showtime*
42 Part of TLC
43 Singer Lennox
44 Flash Gordon portrayer
48 Ending for fin
49 Boom on the briny
50 Hinny's mother
53 "Smile" singer Tony
57 Kind of dog that's not a dog
59 Evita's land: Abbr.
60 Porky Pig's creator
62 Railroad beam
63 Goggle
64 Uncle Vanya's niece
65 Part of HRH
66 Piccadilly Circus statue
67 Nyborg native

DOWN

1 "Have fun!"
2 Shower sponge
3 Like NFL linemen
4 *Legally Blonde* heroine
5 Footnote word
6 *Scrubs* settings
7 Nursery cries
8 All over
9 Marina
10 Poker table chip
11 "Xing" animal on signs
13 Damascus denizen
15 Marianas ___
18 Chop down
22 Contented cry
25 Mail room machines
27 Sun Yat-___
28 Petal plucker's word
29 School-support org.
30 H.H. Munro
31 Sword with a button
32 Egyptian pyramid, e.g.
33 Moises of baseball
34 1973 Nobel Peace Prize winner
38 Long-nosed fish
39 Tolkien beast
40 Paris–Amsterdam dir.
42 Paparazzi targets
43 2009 *Star Trek* director
45 Go for the bronze?
46 Don't compare these to oranges
47 Theda of silents
50 Field of endeavor
51 Campus demonstration
52 Bristles
53 Soaker's spot
54 Buffalo's county
55 Canvas bag
56 Uphill assistance
58 Big Apple seller?
61 ___-Magnon man

★★★ BrainSnack®—Parking Space

Which car (1-11) is parked incorrectly?

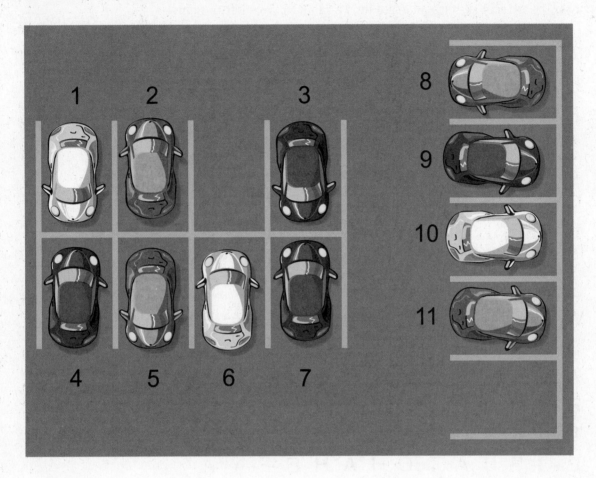

LETTERBLOCKS

Move the letterblocks around so that words are formed on top and below that you can associate with insects.

R * S E I D R
E T C K I C P

★ Agriculture

All the words are hidden vertically, horizontally or diagonally—in both directions. The letters that remain unused form a sentence from left to right.

```
C A G A S P A R A G U S R I C
A U L M T U E R E P R O D U C
R E S A F B O O E L T T A C D
R I A N M T I U R F F S W E L
O L R U A S W O R C E R A C S
T O C R B R E E D I N G N T H
E U R E I G L H O O N W N D S
C S C S U G B C O H E O U L A
V S A U M F A C L R L D A I O
E W U R O E T T H R S A L A P
G B L P O S S Y I I S E F L I
E A I L R W T C R O C M A F N
T R F U H O F O Y E N O I U S
A L L S S C T R M T L L R D R
B E O E U A T C H A H E E Y A
L Y W E M R A N A D T E C B P
E S E M U G E L I R W O O F U
E Y R T L U O P P O T A T O L
```

COWS
CUCUMBER
FENNEL
FLAIL
FRUIT
HORSE
IRRIGATION
LEGUMES
MANURE SURPLUS
MEADOW
MUSHROOM
PARSNIP
POTATO
POULTRY
SCARECROW
SCYTHE
STABLE
TOMATO
TRACTOR
VEGETABLE
WEEDS

ANNUAL FAIR
ASPARAGUS
BARLEY

BREEDING
CARROT
CATTLE

CAULIFLOWER
CELERY
CHICORY

CHANGE ONE

Change one letter in each of these two words to form a common two-word phrase.

ROT BAKES

★★★★★ Weird Al by John M. Samson

ACROSS

1 Diner dish
5 Blue dyes
10 Chinese dynasty
14 Alms box
15 Marisa in *Anger Management*
16 Flat fee
17 "Are you for ___?"
18 Windows font
19 Wheel shaft
20 "Weird Al" parody of a Lady Gaga song
23 Capital of Washington
24 Coal dust
25 "___ Triplex": R.L. Stevenson
26 *Gangs of New York* director
30 Gladys Knight's group
33 Make amends
34 Zenith
35 "Weird Al" parody of "Piano Man"
39 Suffix for profit
40 Bank claims
41 ___ and crafts
42 Street through the center of town
44 "Baby Baby" singer Grant
46 Answers a raise
47 Some daisies
51 "Weird Al" parody of an MC Hammer song
54 "Ewww" inducer
55 Copier company
56 Master-at-___
57 "Clue" weapon
58 "How much ___ much?"
59 Mediocre marks
60 Drained sap from
61 Detective Vance
62 "The original sneaker" company

DOWN

1 *Duck Soup* star
2 Dancing giddily
3 À la King
4 Flag position
5 Classic video game systems
6 Desmond in *Sunset Blvd.*
7 "You tagged me!"
8 Remini in *Old School*
9 Grease alternative
10 Barely advances
11 Measure used in the *Iliad*
12 This and no more
13 SUV
21 Unlock, in verse
22 Less iffy
26 Attacked by a bee
27 Long-running FOX reality show
28 Put into piles
29 *Aeneid*, e.g.
30 Maya Angelou work
31 Fresh thought
32 Sub's "eyes"
33 Addled
36 "Here we are as in ___ days ..."
37 Bush pilot's destination
38 Little Boy Blue's sleeping site
43 Approached
44 "Bless you!" elicitor
45 ___-jongg
47 *Cheers* chair
48 Graces' number
49 Drew a bead on
50 Sizzling sound
51 Screen favorite
52 Yearn for
53 *The Book of Mormon* opener
54 Royal symbol

★ Sudoku Twin

Fill in the grid so that each row, each column and each 3 x 3 frame contains every number from 1 to 9. A sudoku twin is two connected 9 x 9 sudokus.

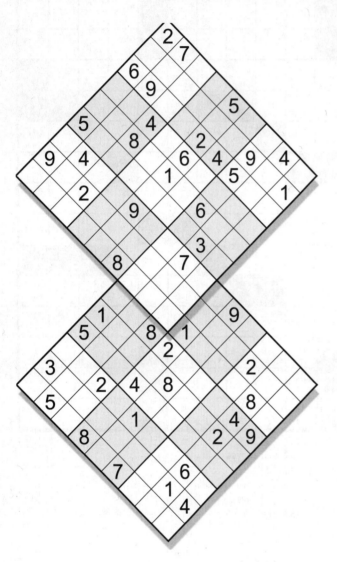

REPOSITION PREPOSITION

Unscramble LONG IDEAS and find a one-word preposition.

★★ Keep Going

Start on a blank square of your choice and connect as many blank squares as possible with one single continuous line. You can only connect squares along vertical and horizontal lines, not along diagonal lines. You must continue the connecting line up until the next obstacle, i.e. the rim of the box, a black square or a square that has already been used. You can change direction at any obstacle you meet. Each square can only be used once. The number of blank squares that will be left unused is marked in the upper square. There is more than one solution. We only show one solution.

DOUBLETALK

What word means "a supporter" or "a unit of time"?

★★★★★ Leading Ladies by John M. Samson

ACROSS

1 Baldwin in *The Marrying Man*
5 Slumbered
10 Cowboy QB Tony
14 Celine Dion, for one
15 Nonconformist
16 Suffix for mod
17 "'Nuff said!"
18 Immigrant from Tokyo
19 *Pretty Woman* actor
20 *Melvin and Howard* Oscar winner
23 "___ la-la!"
24 Dos Passos trilogy
25 Bass lure
29 Erstwhile
33 El Dorado treasure
34 Potter's friend Hermione
36 ___ de plume
37 Rolling Stones album
38 Airport near Tel Aviv
39 Jungfrau, for one
40 "Rose ___ rose ..."
41 Eight-pointed cross
45 "Unforgettable" King Cole
46 Buick or Toyota model
48 Preschool school
50 Tread the boards
51 LI doubled
52 *He Loves Me* star
61 White House room
62 Reddish purple
63 Stanley Gardner
64 Satanic
65 "Primitive" feelings
66 Nothing, in Barcelona
67 ___ majesty
68 Prophets
69 Russian imperialist

DOWN

1 Sandler in *Grown Ups*
2 Peru's "City of the Kings"
3 Whom ender
4 A river runs through it
5 Act like a snake
6 "Heads I win, tails you ___"
7 Mass. motto word
8 Hammer end
9 Horace Greeley's newspaper
10 Ankle biter
11 Designer Cassini
12 Black Beauty's mom
13 Ishii of *Kill Bill* films
21 Jimmy Webb creation
22 Software purchaser
25 "America's Drive-In" chain
26 "Purple" writing
27 Des Moines denizen
28 Come from behind
29 Marie Osmond's birthplace
30 Pointless
31 Back tooth
32 Running on fumes
35 "___ a problem!"
41 "Don't Get Around ___ Anymore"
42 19th-century humorist Ward
43 Happy outcome
44 *CHiPS* star Estrada
47 Act the rat
49 Reticent
52 "Mind me, Rover!"
53 Trough locale
54 "Buyer beware" phrase
55 Like the Florida panther
56 Speedy sled
57 CB sign-off
58 La Belle Epoch et al.
59 Alan in *The Aviator*
60 Posterior

★ Monkey Business

Some of the older students have been monkeying about with the BEST KIDS BOOKS titles list in the library. Can you fix it?

CHANGE ONE

Change one letter in each of these two words to form a common two-word phrase.

FIGHT FEAR

★ Word Pyramid

Each word in the pyramid has the letters of the word above it, plus a new letter.

T
(1) point in time
(2) insect living in organized colonies
(3) volcano in Sicily
(4) broker
(5) feeding
(6) make hot
(7) instructing

TRANSADDITION

Add one letter to I COUNTED and rearrange the rest to find a connection.

★★★★★ Best-Sellers I by John M. Samson

ACROSS

1 Poor golf shot
5 First Family daughter
10 Wasteland
14 Three oceans touch it
15 Jordan capital
16 "You ___": Lady Gaga
17 Nora Roberts best-seller
19 Jockey's strap
20 Balance providers
21 Decent, so to speak
23 Salad green
24 *From Here to Eternity* island
25 *The Water Horse* loch
27 Folic acid, for one
30 Rough finish
33 2000 election hangers
35 Jane Smiley best-seller
36 You've heard this before
37 Harvests
38 Head of France
39 Notice
40 Fauvist Matisse
41 Sea fan
42 1946 Triple Crown horse
44 Beat bad
46 Sea eagle
47 Kind of energy
51 Henry Fonda western (with *The*)
54 Pizza spice
55 As far as
56 Elin Hilderbrand best-seller
58 "___ to Run": Springsteen
59 Online letter
60 Work without ___ (risk it)
61 Ice-cream brand
62 "My Heart Belongs to ___"
63 Beatty and Flanders

DOWN

1 Juice the goose
2 Colorado ski spot
3 Kind of hockey
4 ___ line (conform)
5 Buffalo team
6 "Girl" singer Tori
7 Dallas school
8 Worker
9 Robots
10 *Nick of Time* actress Mason
11 David Baldacci best-seller
12 *Garfield* canine
13 Peel
18 "American Pie" destination
22 Café sign
26 Perfume
27 Bland
28 9th Greek letter
29 "Away in a Manger" is one
30 Rimrock
31 Gets a serve past
32 Robert Crais best-seller
34 Laughter sound
37 Allowed to go
38 Bobsled relative
40 Track down
41 More adorable
43 Illegal ignitions
45 Almost never
48 Boothbay Harbor locale
49 "Lady ___": Chris de Burgh
50 Indianapolis team
51 London subway
52 Apple product
53 *Green Mansions* girl
54 *Amores* poet
57 Schoolboy

★★ Sunny Weather

Where will the sun shine knowing that each arrow points in the direction of a spot where the symbol is located? The symbols cannot be next to each other vertically, horizontally or diagonally. A symbol cannot be placed on top of an arrow. We show one symbol.

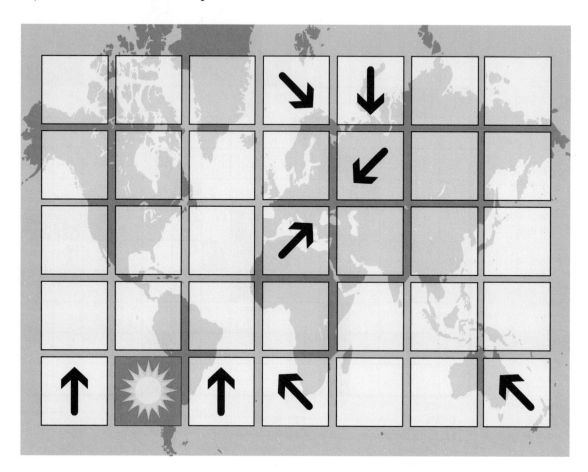

BLOCK ANAGRAM

Form the words that are described in the brackets with the letters above the grid. Extra letters are already in the right place.

MERCILESS (bomb)

| | | U | I | | | | | I | | S | | | |

★★★ BrainSnack®—Flag It

Each signal flag is represented by a letter. Two signal flags strongly resemble each other per column. Which flag does not belong?

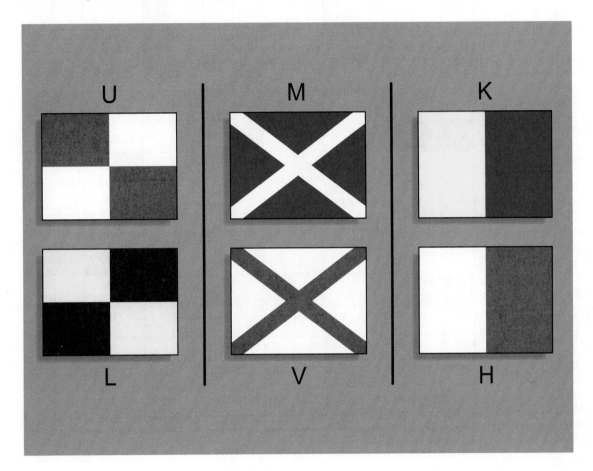

END GAME

The words you are seeking all have the letters END in them in the position indicated. When you have found all of the answers, from the clues on the right, one column will reveal the END GAME word which might take till the cows come home.

_	_	_	_	_	E	N	D	To protect or ward off
_	_	_	E	N	D	_	_	Disburser
_	_	_	E	N	D	_	_	A body of stories
E	N	D	_	_	_	_	_	Growth from within

★★★★★ Best-Sellers II by John M. Samson

ACROSS

1 "Please respond"
5 Florida citrus center
10 Bushy hairstyle
14 Buckeye State
15 Name on a check
16 Office wear
17 Tina Fey best-seller
19 Shutter strip
20 Beach shrinkage
21 Board game with discs
23 Round robin
24 Sage, e.g.
25 Shaped glass
27 "Day Tripper" group
30 Kiddie
33 Butler of fiction
35 "Hail, Caesar!"
36 Like a blue moon
37 Round bread loaf
38 A tug may tow it
39 1969 Nobel Peace Prize gp.
40 Areca nut
41 "Monopoly" ship, e.g.
42 Pep-rally blaze
44 Big-budget film
46 Cod cousin
47 *Super 8* director
51 Cataclysmic
54 Balkan state
55 12th Hebrew month
56 Jim Butcher best-seller
58 Stand up
59 Scary
60 *Lord of the Rings* creatures
61 "___ there, done that!"
62 O'Reilly of *M*A*S*H*
63 Area below Greenwich Village

DOWN

1 Graduation wear
2 Seaboard
3 Baseball cap part
4 Workable
5 Act against
6 *Brian's Song* Emmy nominee
7 *Anthem* author Rand
8 *American Psycho* actor Jared
9 Affected lover of beauty
10 Affirm
11 Brad Thor best-seller
12 100 Iranian dinars
13 *A Fish Called Wanda* character
18 Road sign
22 Qualifying race
26 Penned
27 *Beauty and the Beast* beauty
28 Ancient cry of revelry
29 Stitched
30 Nursery bed
31 Sundog
32 John Hart best-seller
34 Color
37 Tom in *Major League*
38 "Know thyself" philosopher
40 Schwinn product
41 *They Call Me MISTER ___* (1970)
43 Conquered
45 Be deceitful
48 "That's ___!" ("Don't do that!")
49 Amusement
50 Final authority
51 Action word
52 Nastase of tennis
53 "Take ___ Train"
54 Large land mass
57 O'Hare airport code

★★ The Puzzled Librarian

The new library assistant accidentally bumped into the Good Reads notice board, and the magnetic letters all fell off. The librarian remembered the authors' names, but needs some help to get the titles right, as the chief librarian will be back in ten minutes!

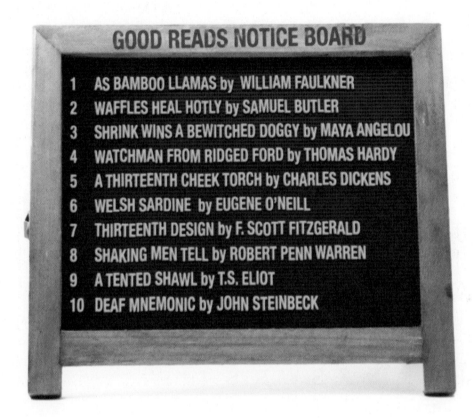

GOOD READS NOTICE BOARD

1 AS BAMBOO LLAMAS by WILLIAM FAULKNER
2 WAFFLES HEAL HOTLY by SAMUEL BUTLER
3 SHRINK WINS A BEWITCHED DOGGY by MAYA ANGELOU
4 WATCHMAN FROM RIDGED FORD by THOMAS HARDY
5 A THIRTEENTH CHEEK TORCH by CHARLES DICKENS
6 WELSH SARDINE by EUGENE O'NEILL
7 THIRTEENTH DESIGN by F. SCOTT FITZGERALD
8 SHAKING MEN TELL by ROBERT PENN WARREN
9 A TENTED SHAWL by T.S. ELIOT
10 DEAF MNEMONIC by JOHN STEINBECK

MISSING LETTER PROVERB

Fill in each missing letter, indicated by an X, to make a well-known proverb.

XIXHT XIXE XITH XIXE

★ Photography

All the words are hidden vertically, horizontally or diagonally—in both directions. The letters that remain unused form a sentence from left to right.

```
S L I D E P R O J E C T O R T
E U Q I N H C E T H M O D E L
E V M W E D A L B L E S S A H
P I E D N O M M R D P H O A T
I G G E L O E G O R A P H M Y
R N A V A T R I P O D I S A D
T E P E R E A O R I R V E R D
S T I L G F R L S R O K M O G
T T X O E T A U R E E K R N I
C I E P R T C X A L L A R A P
A N L A I O N A T U R E T P D
T G I G F L Z O O M L E N S I
N T I O T E R T H G I L A L L
O D T Y M E F A N X S W R S I
C U T S A T E L L I T E N I F
A P E R T U R E A F N E G I W
S H A R P N E S S S L I L T H
E V I T A G E N L I H M G H T
```

MODEL
NATURE
NEGATIVE
PANORAMA
PARALLAX
PORTRAIT
SATELLITE
SHARPNESS
SLIDE PROJECTOR
TECHNIQUE
TRIPOD
VIGNETTING
ZOOM LENS

APERTURE
AUTOFOCUS
CAMERA
CONTACT STRIP
DARKROOM

DEVELOP
DIGITAL
ENLARGER
FILM
FIX

FLASH
HASSELBLAD
LENS
LIGHT
MEGAPIXEL

DELETE ONE

Delete one letter from TRUE REFLECTION and rearrange the rest to find a copier.

★ Cage the Animals

Draw lines to completely divide up the grid into small squares with exactly one animal per square. The squares should not overlap.

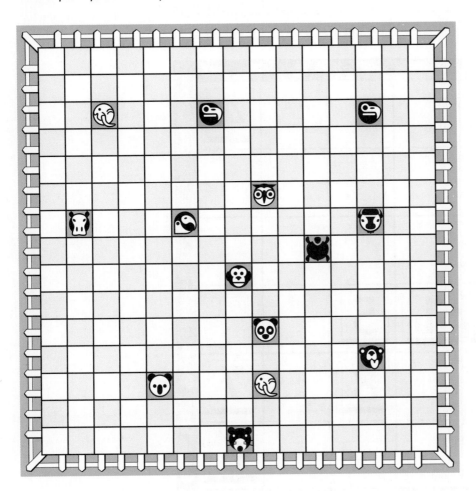

CHANGELINGS

Each of the three lines of letters below should spell words which have a food connection. The letters have been mixed up. Four letters from the first word are now in the third line, four letters from the third word are in the second line and four letters from the second word are in the first line. The remaining letters are in their original places. What are the words?

V A G N E T L B N I
P E I E S A R L E S
C A T N S L E O I E

★★ Number Cluster

Complete the grid by constituting adjoining clusters that consist of as many cubes as the number on the cubes. At cube 5, for instance, you will have to make a five-cube cluster. Two or more figure cubes of the same value belong to the same cluster. You can only place your cubes along horizontal and/or vertical lines.

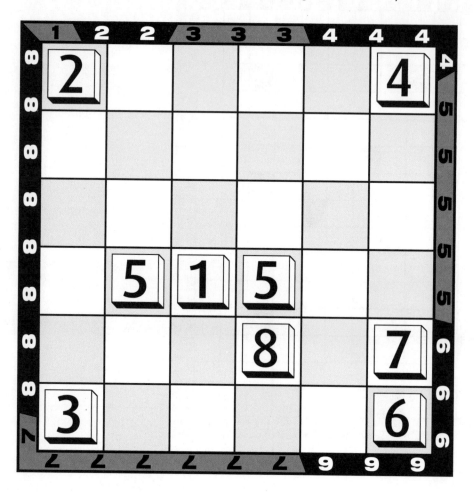

LETTER LINE

Put a letter in each of the squares below to make a word which describes "mechanical devices." These numbered clues refer to other words which can be made from the whole.

**1 8 5 4 6 7 2 MASTER; 6 8 1 9 5 7 MEDDLE;
4 6 7 5 8 1 RIVER; 1 8 4 6 5 7 KEEPER.**

1	2	3	4	5	6	7	8	9	10

★ Spot the Differences

Find the nine differences in the image on the right.

DELETE ONE

Delete one letter from STUPID TALES and rearrange the rest to find calm.

★★★★★ Relaxation by Sam Bellotto Jr.

ACROSS

1 Scored 1 at Sawgrass
5 Like Presley's early records
9 *Enola Gay* cargo
14 Petty in *Free Willy*
15 Auction site
16 Gaffer's milieu
17 First element of a perfect summer's day
20 Gibson garnish
21 ___ loss for words
22 Juice bar orders
23 Itch
26 All tied
28 Second element of a perfect summer's day
33 Some are liberal
34 Astral altar
35 Superman, on Krypton
37 Super Sunday shout
38 Hickman and Johnson
41 *Die Fledermaus* role
42 Kunta of *Roots*
44 "Star Spangled Banner" preposition
45 Wolf relatives
46 Third element of a perfect summer's day
50 Concept
51 Gumbo pod
52 Richard in *Gog*
55 Vex
57 Single-celled protozoan
61 Fourth element of a perfect summer's day
65 Niger's neighbor
66 Of the ear
67 Patricia in *Hud*
68 Like Splenda
69 "Here ___ again!"
70 James Bond foe

DOWN

1 A chorus line
2 Joe McCarthy's counsel
3 "Able was I ___ ..."
4 Cuts out of the will
5 Game pieces
6 Japanese sash
7 *Pioneer 10* org.
8 Bluepoint
9 Cannes chum
10 Mother lode
11 "Ibis" poet
12 Tunnel
13 Panhandles
18 The U of CPU
19 One not in need
24 Deli salad
25 Greek Juno
27 Cries in balloons
28 Galahad's quest
29 Culture: Comb. form
30 Sluggish inlet
31 G-man Ness
32 Rushlike
33 Ham's refuge
36 ___ Palmas
38 Legal paper
39 Pixar clownfish
40 Composer Satie
43 Hostess snack cake
45 April birthstone
47 Bridle attachment
48 Jean in *Bombshell*
49 Apothecary's weight
52 Recedes
53 Escalated
54 Superb
56 Winslet in *Contagion*
58 Pitcher
59 Noodle
60 1968 folk album
62 "Say ah" clinic
63 Censure
64 Sarge

PAGE 15

Pet Cats

O	L	A	F		C	U	B	I	C		S	T	E	T
S	O	H	O		A	R	E	N	A		T	H	I	S
A	G	A	R		M	A	N	O	F		O	O	N	A
G	A	R	F	I	E	L	D		F	A	R	M	E	R
E	N	D	E	A	R	S		S	E	L	M	A		
		I	N	A		T	H	I	E	S	S	E	N	
M	I	S	T	S		S	E	I	N	E		I	L	A
R	O	Y	S		B	L	A	R	E		S	N	A	P
E	L	L		A	L	E	R	T		S	C	A	L	E
D	E	V	E	L	O	P	S		A	L	A			
		E	X	I	S	T		S	T	A	B	L	E	S
T	A	S	T	E	S		S	N	O	W	B	A	L	L
E	N	T	E		O	F	T	E	N		A	T	E	E
A	T	E	N		M	E	L	E	E		R	E	N	E
M	A	R	T		S	W	O	R	D		D	R	A	T

PAGE 16

Number Cluster

4	5	7	7	7	7
4	5	3	7	7	7
4	5	3	3	8	8
4	5	5	8	8	6
2	2	8	8	6	6
1	8	8	6	6	6

ONE LETTER LESS OR MORE
INHALER

PAGE 17

BrainSnack®—Touchdown

The digits of the scores of the two teams always form a consecutive series. For the last score this is 0, 1, 2.

UNCANNY TURN
TELEVISION NEWS

PAGE 18

Pet Dogs

B	R	O	M		A	S	C	O	T		E	S	P	Y
R	A	V	I		S	P	A	N	O		N	C	A	A
E	D	E	N		C	L	A	I	M		T	O	U	R
E	I	N	S	T	E	I	N		H	A	R	O	L	D
D	I	S	T	A	N	T		C	A	L	E	B		
			R	I	T		C	O	N	V	E	Y	E	D
C	A	M	E	L		E	R	I	K	A		D	R	E
A	G	A	L		M	I	E	N	S		L	O	A	M
R	U	R		T	I	D	E	S		K	Y	O	T	O
R	E	M	A	I	N	E	D		H	E	R			
		A	D	L	E	R		S	E	N	I	O	R	S
L	A	D	D	E	R		S	P	R	O	C	K	E	T
E	L	U	L		A	L	A	R	M		I	A	M	A
N	I	K	E		L	I	K	E	A		S	P	A	R
S	E	E	D		S	T	E	E	N		T	I	N	T

PAGE 19

U.S.A.

The name America is probably derived from Amerigo Vespucci, a merchant and sailor who was born in Florence.

CHANGE ONE
SWITCH ON

PAGE 20

Keep Going

FRIENDS
Each can have the prefix ARCH- to form a new word.

PAGE 21

2011 Movies I

C	A	R	T		S	C	R	A	M		P	L	E	D
A	S	O	R		P	R	I	M	A		R	I	V	A
C	I	A	O		L	E	A	S	T		E	M	I	L
H	A	L	L	P	A	S	S		E	A	S	I	L	Y
E	N	D	L	E	S	S		T	R	I	T	T		
			I	S	H		G	O	N	D	O	L	A	S
B	I	Z	E	T		U	L	N	A	E		E	B	O
A	D	O	S		F	L	A	I	L		O	S	L	O
L	E	O		S	E	E	N	O		A	S	S	E	T
L	A	K	E	L	A	N	D		A	H	S			
		E	V	E	R	T		T	R	A	I	N	E	D
B	R	E	A	D	S		F	A	S	T	F	I	V	E
L	A	P	D		O	H	A	R	E		I	T	E	M
O	G	E	E		M	E	L	O	N		E	R	N	O
B	A	R	D		E	L	A	T	E		D	O	T	S

PAGE 22

Sudoku

5	3	1	6	4	9	2	8	7
4	6	2	5	8	7	1	9	3
9	7	8	2	1	3	5	4	6
7	8	4	3	5	6	9	2	1
2	9	6	1	7	8	4	3	5
1	5	3	9	2	4	7	6	8
8	4	9	7	3	5	6	1	2
6	2	5	8	9	1	3	7	4
3	1	7	4	6	2	8	5	9

DOODLE PUZZLE
MiddleWeight

PAGE 23

Sport Maze

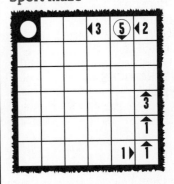

ONE LETTER LESS OR MORE
CHOLERA

PAGE 24
2011 Movies II

A	R	E	S		S	M	U	G		E	S	S	E	N
N	A	L	A		T	A	T	E		C	H	O	R	E
T	H	E	B	E	A	V	E	R		S	O	U	S	E
E	S	C	O	R	T	S		M	A	T	U	R	E	D
			T	O	I			T	A	L	C			
T	A	B	A	S	C	O		M	I	S	D	E	E	D
A	R	A	G	E		D	R	I	L	Y		C	U	R
L	O	D	E		H	E	I	S	T		S	O	R	A
E	S	T		B	E	T	T	E		S	Y	D	O	W
S	E	E	S	A	W	S		R	E	P	R	E	S	S
		A	C	R	E			R	E	A				
R	E	C	O	R	D	S		M	A	R	C	E	A	U
O	C	H	R	E		T	H	E	S	M	U	R	F	S
C	R	E	E	L		L	A	D	E		S	I	R	E
K	U	R	D	S		O	D	O	R		E	N	O	S

PAGE 27
Best of Bob

T	R	I	B		S	E	R	A	C		C	C	C	P
H	I	C	E		C	L	O	T	H		A	L	A	I
A	A	A	A		H	O	U	R	I		M	O	S	T
I	T	H	R	E	W	I	T	A	L	L	A	W	A	Y
S	A	N	C	T	A			D	O	R	N			
			L	A	N	E		M	I	T	O	S	I	S
R	I	T	A			L	E	A	S	T		U	N	O
B	L	O	W	I	N	I	N	T	H	E	W	I	N	D
I	S	M		F	E	A	S	T			I	T	S	A
S	E	A	B	E	D	S		E	D	E	N			
			R	E	E	K			E	R	E	C	T	S
T	A	N	G	L	E	D	U	P	I	N	B	L	U	E
A	T	O	I		L	I	L	A	C		A	I	M	E
K	O	L	N		L	E	A	S	E		R	C	M	P
E	N	D	S		Y	U	R	T	S		S	K	Y	S

PAGE 30
Themeless

H	U	R	T		S	T	A	S	H		A	H	S	O
O	N	E	R		P	I	N	T	O		L	E	T	S
R	I	P	E		L	E	G	U	P		L	A	R	A
S	T	R	A	Y	E	D		D	E	M	E	T	E	R
T	S	E	T	S	E			L	I	G	H	T		
			S	I	E	N	A		B	E	S	E	E	C	H
A	M	E	E	R		T	O	A	S	T		R	H	O
M	E	N	S		C	L	A	S	S		A	L	E	S
I	T	T		K	H	A	K	I		S	N	O	R	E
R	E	A	P	E	R	S		C	O	L	I	C		
		O	T	A	R	Y			B	A	S	K	E	T
B	R	I	T	I	S	H		J	E	W	E	L	R	Y
R	I	V	E		L	E	R	O	Y		T	E	A	K
A	T	E	N		E	R	O	D	E		T	A	T	E
C	E	S	T		R	A	B	I	D		E	R	O	S

PAGE 25
Word Sudoku

E	U	G	M	I	S	A	T	Z
A	S	M	T	Z	E	G	I	U
Z	I	T	G	A	U	M	S	E
S	E	A	I	T	G	Z	U	M
I	G	U	E	M	Z	S	A	T
M	T	Z	S	U	A	E	G	I
G	M	S	U	E	I	T	Z	A
T	Z	I	A	S	M	U	E	G
U	A	E	Z	G	T	I	M	S

SANDWICH
SLEEP

PAGE 26
BrainSnack®—Crazy Cube

Solution:
Block 7.

LETTERBLOCKS
BATTERY
OPENING

PAGE 28
Binairo

0	1	1	0	0	1	1	0	1	0	1	0
1	0	1	0	1	0	0	1	0	1	0	1
0	1	0	1	0	1	1	0	0	1	0	1
0	0	1	0	1	1	0	1	1	0	1	0
1	1	0	1	0	0	1	0	1	0	0	1
1	0	0	1	0	0	1	1	0	1	1	0
0	1	1	0	1	1	0	0	1	0	1	0
1	0	0	1	1	0	1	0	0	1	0	1
0	0	1	0	0	1	0	1	1	0	1	1
1	1	0	0	1	0	0	1	1	0	1	0
1	0	1	1	0	1	1	0	0	1	0	0
0	1	0	1	1	0	0	1	0	1	0	1

REPOSITION PREPOSITION
IN ADDITION TO

PAGE 29
Spot the Differences

DOUBLETALK
ENTRANCE

PAGE 31
Cage the Animals

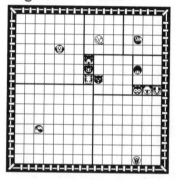

TRANSADDITION
Add S and find TELEVISION PROGRAMMING

PAGE 32
Jazz

Jazz music originated at the beginning of the twentieth century amongst dance orchestras in New Orleans.

MISSING LETTER PROVERB
Cleanliness is next to godliness.

PAGE 33

Sunny Weather

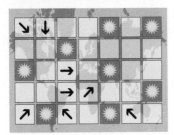

BLOCK ANAGRAM

IRONING BOARD

PAGE 34

Sleuths

S	C	O	P		S	H	A	R	P		S	L	A	W
I	R	A	E		P	O	L	A	R		L	E	D	A
M	I	S	S	M	A	R	P	L	E		O	W	E	N
B	E	T	T	E	R	S		E	L	E	G	A	N	T
A	S	S	E	T	S			A	D	A	R			
	R	E	E	K		S	T	E	N	C	I	L		
T	O	N	E	R		R	I	P	E	N		H	O	E
A	P	E	D		H	E	R	E	S		S	E	N	T
L	A	R		I	O	W	A	N		M	A	R	A	T
C	H	O	R	T	L	E		D	I	A	L			
		W	A	S	I			S	H	E	R	P	A	
A	V	O	C	A	D	O		F	L	A	S	H	E	S
D	A	L	I		A	D	R	I	A	N	M	O	N	K
A	L	F	A		Y	E	A	R	N		A	N	N	E
H	E	E	L		S	A	T	E	D		N	E	E	D

PAGE 35

Kakuro

7	4	8			7	8	9
	1	3			5	4	
8	7	9	5			7	4
5			8	7	6		
		6	1	2			
1	2	3			9	8	7
3	7					7	1

ONE LETTER LESS OR MORE

SINCERE

PAGE 36

BrainSnack®—Pedal Power

Glove 6. 5 and 6 are both right-hand gloves. The left-hand gloves always have the letters ABC and the right-hand gloves have CBA.

END GAME

D I V I D E N D
E N D P O I N T
B L E N D I N G
T E N D E R L Y

PAGE 37

College Teams

L	I	B	R	A		H	A	L	F		A	L	A	E
I	S	L	E	S		A	M	O	R		M	O	S	S
S	E	U	S	S		G	A	M	E	C	O	C	K	S
P	R	E	C	E	D	E	D		S	I	N	I	S	E
	D	U	R	A	N		S	H	A	G				
S	H	E	E	T	S		G	A	L	O	S	H	E	S
M	A	V	S		H	A	R	D	Y		T	U	R	N
E	L	I		C	I	A			R	N	A			
A	L	L	S		M	A	T	T	E		G	R	I	P
R	E	S	T	L	E	S	S		S	E	R	I	E	S
			R	I	L	E		M	A	N	I	C		
S	H	E	I	L	A		P	O	I	G	N	A	N	T
C	A	R	D	I	N	A	L	S		A	N	N	I	E
A	L	I	E		I	R	A	E		G	E	E	N	A
T	E	S	S		E	F	T	S		E	D	S	E	L

PAGE 38

Keep Going

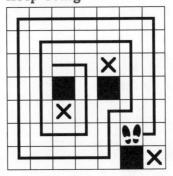

DELETE ONE

Delete A and find SORE THROAT

PAGE 39

Sudoku

6	3	7	9	5	8	4	1	2
1	4	2	7	6	3	8	5	9
8	5	9	4	1	2	3	7	6
5	7	8	1	2	6	9	3	4
4	1	6	3	9	5	7	2	8
2	9	3	8	7	4	1	6	5
3	2	4	5	8	1	6	9	7
7	8	5	6	3	9	2	4	1
9	6	1	2	4	7	5	8	3

CHANGELINGS

L I G H T H O U S E
C O A S T G U A R D
S H I P W R E C K S

PAGE 40

Play Ball!

R	I	F	L	E		B	A	I	T		F	R	A	T
A	R	I	E	S		A	S	S	E		A	U	T	O
M	A	R	A	T		S	H	O	R	T	S	T	O	P
A	E	S	T	H	E	T	E		M	O	T	T	L	E
	T	H	E	R	E		B	I	G	E	Y	E	D	
R	O	B	E	R	T		S	A	T	A	N			
O	M	A	R		E	N	U	R	E		S	H	U	N
O	A	S		A	N	E				O	S	E		
K	N	E	E		H	O	U	S	E		A	M	E	N
			S	T	A	M	P		S	E	V	E	R	E
M	A	R	C	O	N	I		S	T	R	O	P		
E	C	H	O	E	D		A	M	A	R	I	L	L	O
T	H	I	R	D	B	A	S	E		A	D	A	I	R
R	E	N	T		A	R	I	L		T	E	T	R	A
O	D	E	S		G	E	N	T		A	D	E	A	L

PAGE 41

Sport Maze

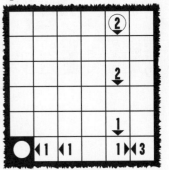

LETTER LINE

INTRODUCE; REDUCTION, INDUCE, CONDUIT, RUINED

PAGE 42

Word Sudoku

A	K	D	R	C	E	O	S	P
S	E	O	K	P	A	C	D	R
C	P	R	S	O	D	K	E	A
P	S	E	O	A	R	D	K	C
D	A	K	E	S	C	R	P	O
R	O	C	D	K	P	E	A	S
O	C	S	P	E	K	A	R	D
E	R	P	A	D	O	S	C	K
K	D	A	C	R	S	P	O	E

ONE LETTER LESS OR MORE
AMAZING

PAGE 43

BrainSnack®—Shirt Number

140. A red circle = 100, gray = 50, black = 10 and white = 1. The last shirt reads 100 + 50 -10 = 140.

UNCANNY TURN
SPECIAL RECIPE

PAGE 44

Potpourri

H	A	A	S		D	E	A	L	S		A	D	O	S
A	M	M	O		I	N	G	O	T		R	E	P	O
R	A	U	L		S	T	O	N	E		A	P	E	R
T	H	R	E	E	L	E	G	G	E	D	R	A	C	E
			M	C	I				P	E	A	R		
R	O	A	N	O	K	E		F	L	A	T	T	E	N
I	B	N		L	E	V	E	L	E	D		M	E	A
L	E	T			E	T	A			E	R	I		
E	L	I		S	T	R	E	T	C	H		N	I	A
D	I	S	T	O	R	T		T	O	A	S	T	E	D
	O	O	L	A				S	I	P				
J	A	C	K	O	F	A	L	L	T	R	A	D	E	S
A	L	I	I		F	R	E	O	N		C	O	I	N
G	O	A	L		I	N	A	N	E		E	N	N	A
S	E	L	L		C	O	R	E	R		D	E	E	P

PAGE 45

Cage the Animals

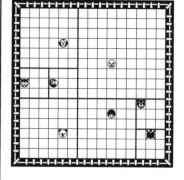

DOODLE PUZZLE
CountDown

PAGE 46

Binairo

I	O	O	I	I	O	O	I	I	O	I
I	I	O	I	O	O	I	O	I	I	O
O	I	I	O	I	I	O	I	O	I	O
I	O	I	I	O	O	I	I	O	O	I
O	I	O	I	O	I	I	O	I	I	O
O	O	I	O	I	I	O	I	I	O	I
I	I	O	I	I	O	I	O	O	I	O
O	I	I	O	O	I	I	O	I	O	I
I	O	I	O	I	I	O	I	O	I	O
I	O	O	I	O	O	I	I	O	I	I
O	I	I	O	I	I	O	O	I	O	I

CHANGE ONE
HUMBLE PIE

PAGE 47

Low Points

S	T	A	G		F	O	L	I	C		E	L	A	N
L	I	D	A		A	L	U	L	A		L	U	K	E
O	A	H	U		U	L	N	A	R		I	L	I	A
G	R	A	N	D	C	A	N	Y	O	N	J	U	M	P
S	A	N	T	E	E			L	E	A				
			L	P	T	S		B	I	G	H	O	R	N
I	S	L	E	T		T	E	E	N			L	A	E
D	E	A	T	H	V	A	L	L	E	Y	D	A	Y	S
E	M	I			A	R	A	L		E	A	V	E	S
S	E	R	P	E	N	T		O	R	A	N			
			A	N	I			U	R	S	U	L	A	
V	A	L	L	E	S	M	A	R	I	N	E	R	I	S
E	V	I	L		H	A	G	E	N		U	G	L	I
S	O	L	E		E	L	A	T	E		S	E	L	A
T	W	I	T		D	A	R	E	D		E	D	E	N

PAGE 48

BrainSnack®—Fall Colors

5. There are 5 different shapes of leaves in various fall colors.

BLOCK ANAGRAM
LOS ANGELES

PAGE 49

Cars

R	I	N	C	R	D	R	A	O	B	H	S	A	D	N
O	E	T	A	R	S	B	U	M	P	E	R	I	N	O
O	W	H	E	E	L	L	G	L	G	N	N	U	T	
D	H	G	Y	D	Y	E	S	T	R	T	R	I	M	S
I	E	I	D	N	S	S	C	T	E	R	U	O	E	I
N	E	L	O	I	V	E	C	O	U	P	E	R	H	P
I	L	E	B	L	N	I	K	R	C	R	O	N	B	P
M	S	K	E	Y	N	D	I	A	O	H	A	E	O	
L	L	A	A	C	G	W	T	R	A	D	D	S	F	
M	I	R	R	O	R	A	X	A	E	N	N	U	A	
C	E	B	C	A	R	I	B	D	A	L	C	M	C	A
N	U	F	A	C	D	T	L	R	S	O	U	R	H	
E	R	S	T	A	O	E	L	O	I	O	O	K	F	O
S	P	A	R	K	P	L	U	G	R	A	L	R	A	L
T	E	R	N	A	S	T	L	E	B	T	A	E	S	T
I	V	T	A	E	S	K	C	A	B	E	N	S	O	U
R	P	M	A	L	G	O	F	C	E	S	T	O	F	E
N	E	T	H	E	A	D	L	I	G	H	T	R	G	Y

Increasingly stricter environmental laws force car manufacturers to look for alternative sources of energy.

FRIENDS

Each can have the prefix EXTRA- to form a new word.

PAGE 50

High Points

S	A	L	S		S	H	E	L	F		T	H	A	W
H	A	E	C		H	E	R	E	I		R	O	S	E
A	R	T	E		A	R	I	A	L		A	L	T	A
M	O	U	N	T	W	A	S	H	I	N	G	T	O	N
U	N	S	E	A	L			P	O	I				
			O	R	S	K		P	I	N	C	H	E	D
S	T	I	N	T		E	D	E	N			A	A	A
P	I	K	E	S	P	E	A	K	O	R	B	U	S	T
A	D	E			E	N	N	E		O	U	T	T	A
M	E	A	S	U	R	E		S	P	A	S			
			A	H	S				S	C	R	A	P	E
H	E	A	D	F	O	R	T	H	E	H	I	L	L	S
E	N	I	D		N	O	Y	O	U		D	E	A	N
L	O	D	E		A	S	E	E	D		E	V	I	E
P	L	A	N		L	A	S	S	O		S	E	T	S

PAGE 51

Keep Going

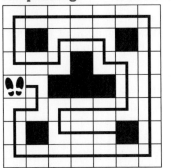

REPOSITION PREPOSITION

IN ACCORDANCE WITH

PAGE 52

Sudoku

2	9	3	6	5	8	7	1	4
5	7	1	4	3	9	8	2	6
6	8	4	1	2	7	5	9	3
7	3	5	9	8	6	1	4	2
4	1	6	5	7	2	3	8	9
8	2	9	3	4	1	6	5	7
9	6	8	2	1	3	4	7	5
1	4	2	7	6	5	9	3	8
3	5	7	8	9	4	2	6	1

SANDWICH

SHIP

PAGE 53

Entomology Exam I

H	A	L	E		S	H	E	B		A	B	B	O	T
A	N	E	T		A	E	R	O		L	E	O	N	A
H	O	N	E	Y	B	E	E	S		F	A	L	C	O
A	N	D	R	O	I	D		C	I	R	C	L	E	S
			N	U	N			M	E	O	W			
A	S	P	I	R	E	R		M	A	D	N	E	S	S
S	T	A	T	E		I	M	A	G	O		E	T	H
C	O	P	Y		E	D	U	C	E		E	V	O	E
A	L	E		M	A	G	M	A		K	L	I	N	E
P	E	R	M	U	T	E		W	H	E	E	L	E	R
	W	A	R	E			E	L	M					
P	R	A	L	I	N	E		D	I	S	E	A	S	E
A	I	S	L	E		D	R	A	G	O	N	F	L	Y
I	M	P	E	L		E	A	C	H		T	R	E	E
L	A	S	T	S		N	Y	E	T		S	O	D	S

PAGE 54

Word Sudoku

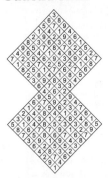

C	W	I	U	B	E	R	T	O
B	O	E	R	C	T	U	I	W
R	T	U	W	I	O	C	B	E
E	C	R	T	O	B	W	U	I
T	B	O	I	U	W	E	R	C
I	U	W	C	E	R	T	O	B
O	R	B	E	W	U	I	C	T
W	I	T	B	R	C	O	E	U
U	E	C	O	T	I	B	W	R

LETTERBLOCKS

BAGPIPE
TRUMPET

PAGE 55

Sport Maze

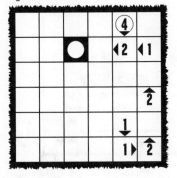

DOUBLETALK

OBJECT

PAGE 56

Entomology Exam II

T	A	T	A		S	W	I	T		S	E	W	E	D
U	R	I	S		C	I	A	O		C	L	O	V	E
B	U	T	T	E	R	F	L	Y		A	A	R	O	N
A	M	O	E	B	A	E		S	T	R	I	K	E	S
			R	E	P			W	I	N	E			
A	D	M	I	R	E	D		M	I	N	E	R	A	L
R	O	O	S	T		O	R	A	N	G		A	T	E
D	U	S	K		B	R	I	N	E		A	N	O	N
E	S	Q		G	R	A	N	T		A	N	T	O	N
N	E	U	T	R	A	L		A	M	N	E	S	T	Y
			I	R	A	N		E	S	C				
A	R	T	I	S	T	S		N	E	E	D	L	E	S
L	O	O	P	S		C	O	C	K	R	O	A	C	H
S	T	E	L	E		A	R	A	L		T	H	O	U
O	A	S	E	S		B	R	A	Y		E	R	N	E

PAGE 57

BrainSnack®—Star Gazer

Star 8. Stars at the same height have the same color.

TRANSADDITION

Add A and find NATURALIST

PAGE 58

Sudoku Twin

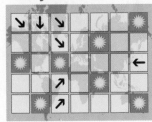

BLOCK ANAGRAM

ACCOUNTANT

PAGE 59

2011 Chart-Toppers

S	E	A	M		A	D	A	M	S		P	S	I	S
A	L	M	A		R	O	B	O	T		H	U	S	H
S	T	E	T		A	L	I	T	O		E	P	E	E
H	O	N	E	Y	B	E	E		M	I	N	E	R	S
A	N	D	R	O	I	D		F	A	V	O	R		
			I	L	A		D	E	C	E	M	B	E	R
S	A	J	A	K		G	O	T	H	S		A	R	O
E	L	U	L		T	A	P	E	S		S	S	N	S
E	D	S		C	R	I	E	D		M	E	S	S	Y
K	I	T	C	H	E	N	S		C	O	E			
	A	R	E	A	S		G	O	O	D	M	A	N	
A	S	K	E	R	S		G	O	O	D	L	I	F	E
W	H	I	P		U	S	U	R	P		E	N	O	S
L	E	S	E		R	I	N	S	E		S	C	O	T
S	A	S	S		E	D	G	E	R		S	E	T	S

PAGE 60

Sunny Weather

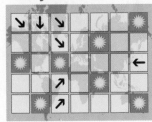

BLOCK ANAGRAM

FOOTBALL PLAYER

PAGE 61

Word Pyramid

A, (1) Ea, (2) sea, (3) sale, (4) lease, (5) asleep, (6) relapse, (7) pleasure

MISSING LETTER PROVERB

All good things must come to an end.

PAGE 62

Cage the Animals

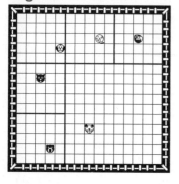

END GAME

INTENDED
FRIENDLY
BENDABLE
UNTENDED

PAGE 63

Actor and Actress

L	A	D	D		M	A	N	O	F		A	G	R	A
A	L	A	I		E	N	N	U	I		V	I	E	D
N	A	N	S		R	E	E	S	E		A	L	F	A
C	R	I	C	K	E	T		T	R	O	L	L	E	Y
E	M	E	R	I	L		C	H	O	I	R			
		L	E	N	Y	A		B	E	R	N	A	R	D
E	R	R	E	D		S	M	I	L	E		N	I	A
C	H	A	T		W	I	T	T	Y		W	A	N	D
R	I	D		S	H	A	V	E		B	I	N	G	O
U	N	C	L	E	A	N		S	C	A	L	D		
	E	L	E	C	T			A	R	L	E	N	E	
T	W	I	S	T	E	R		A	N	D	I	R	O	N
H	I	F	I		V	I	O	L	A		A	S	T	A
I	N	F	O		E	M	B	E	D		M	O	R	T
S	E	E	N		R	A	I	S	A		S	N	E	E

PAGE 64

Binairo

I	O	I	O	I	O	O	I	I	O	O	I
O	I	O	I	I	O	O	I	O	O	I	I
I	O	O	I	O	I	I	O	O	I	I	O
I	O	I	O	O	I	I	O	I	I	O	O
O	I	I	O	I	O	O	I	I	O	O	I
O	I	O	I	O	I	O	I	O	I	I	O
I	O	I	O	I	O	I	O	I	O	O	I
O	I	O	I	O	I	I	O	O	I	I	O
O	I	I	O	I	I	O	O	I	I	O	I
I	O	O	I	O	O	I	I	O	O	I	I
I	I	O	I	O	O	I	I	O	I	I	O
O	O	I	O	I	I	O	O	I	I	O	I

LETTER LINE

CONFISCATE; CAFE, TONICS, FACETS, CONCISE

PAGE 65

Keep Going

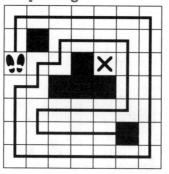

DELETE ONE

Delete one S and find ANCIENTS

PAGE 66

Best in Show

C	U	S	S		B	L	O	C	K		C	A	T	S
O	T	O	H		Y	O	U	R	E		L	U	A	U
M	I	N	I	A	T	U	R	E	P	O	O	D	L	E
P	L	A	N	N	E	R		E	T	H	N	I	C	S
S	E	R	I	N				D	A	T				
			E	A	R	L		O	C	E	L	O	T	S
T	A	D	S		H	O	O	P	L	A		R	I	O
S	C	O	T	T	I	S	H	T	E	R	R	I	E	R
O	R	D		A	N	E	M	I	A		E	A	S	T
S	E	E	D	I	E	R		C	R	A	N			
		C	U	P				N	O	E	L	S		
D	I	A	P	E	R	S		O	U	T	W	A	I	T
E	N	G	L	I	S	H	S	P	R	I	N	G	E	R
A	D	O	E		V	I	R	U	S		E	R	G	O
L	Y	N	X		P	A	I	S	A		D	E	E	P

PAGE 67

BrainSnack®—Seedless

Tannin 1.40%. The sum of the five other percentages equals 100%. Grape pulp does not contain any tannin.

SQUIRCLES

B A A O C B U E
E L E P H A N T
T M R E I L R C
R O A N L L I H
A N T E L O P E
Y D E R Y T E D

PAGE 68

Mathematics

In most languages the word for mathematics is derived from the Greek word máthèma, which means science, knowledge or learning.

ONE LETTER LESS OR MORE

IGNORANCE

PAGE 69

Business Barons I

T	A	M	P		B	O	M	B	E		P	S	T	S
I	B	A	R		E	D	I	E	S		O	A	H	U
R	O	G	E	R	A	I	L	E	S		S	M	E	E
E	D	U	C	A	T	E		F	A	R	A	W	A	Y
D	E	S	I	R	E			Y	O	D	A			
			O	E	N	O		F	I	N	A	L	L	Y
I	M	B	U	E		B	A	L	S	A		T	A	O
D	A	I	S		D	E	P	O	T		S	O	N	G
E	L	L		M	I	S	E	R		R	A	N	D	I
M	E	L	R	O	S	E		A	G	E	R			
	G	E	N	A				A	B	A	C	U	S	
A	N	A	T	O	L	E		P	R	E	S	E	N	T
T	A	T	I		L	E	E	I	A	C	O	C	C	A
L	I	E	N		O	R	A	N	G		T	I	L	L
I	L	S	A		W	O	R	S	E		A	L	E	E

PAGE 70

Number Cluster

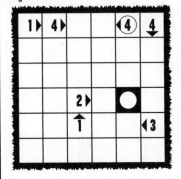

UNCANNY TURN

THE EYES

PAGE 71

BrainSnack®—Skewered

0.30. Six meatballs cost 6 x 2 = 12 sausages. 9 beef cubes cost 9 x 2 = 18 meatballs x 2 = 36 sausages. You pay a total of 16.20 for 12 + 36 + 6 = 54 sausages or 16.20/54 = 0.30 per sausage.

DOODLE PUZZLE

RedUce

PAGE 72

Business Barons II

S	H	A	L	T		T	B	A	R		C	A	T	S
W	A	N	E	S		E	I	N	E		A	R	I	A
A	N	D	I	E		S	T	E	V	E	J	O	B	S
B	A	Y	S	T	A	T	E		E	L	O	P	E	S
		G	U	S	T	Y		G	A	L	L	E	R	Y
G	A	R	R	E	T		Y	A	L	I	E			
O	T	O	E		S	T	E	M	S		D	R	A	G
G	O	V			E	M	U				O	N	O	
O	P	E	C		C	R	E	T	E		A	S	T	O
			L	E	A	N	N		U	N	U	S	E	D
A	P	P	E	A	L	S		C	R	I	S	P		
G	R	E	A	S	Y		E	L	E	C	T	E	E	S
L	A	R	R	Y	P	A	G	E		H	E	R	N	E
E	D	I	E		S	H	A	R		E	R	O	D	E
T	O	L	D		O	I	N	K		S	E	T	O	N

PAGE 73

Sport Maze

CHANGE ONE

GREEN FINGERS

PAGE 74

Word Sudoku

D	T	S	O	J	H	G	U	N
J	O	H	N	G	U	S	D	T
G	N	U	S	D	T	O	H	J
N	H	O	G	S	D	T	J	U
S	U	J	T	H	O	N	G	D
T	G	D	J	U	N	H	S	O
H	S	N	D	T	J	U	O	G
O	J	G	U	N	S	D	T	H
U	D	T	H	O	G	J	N	S

LETTERBLOCKS

BLOSSOM
COMPOST

PAGE 75

Themeless

C	A	R	P		T	R	A	C	T		A	J	A	R
A	G	I	O		R	U	M	O	R		N	E	M	O
S	E	C	T		A	D	I	E	U		G	N	U	S
E	N	H	A	N	C	E		D	E	F	E	N	S	E
S	T	A	T	U	E			B	E	L	I	E		
			R	O	N	D	O		A	L	L	O	F	M	E
H	A	D	E	S		R	A	O	U	L		E	E	L
A	R	M	S		C	A	D	R	E		E	R	N	O
T	R	U		M	O	N	E	T		A	M	A	T	I
H	O	L	D	I	N	G		A	A	R	O	N		
	G	L	E	N	N			B	I	T	I	N	G	
D	A	I	S	I	E	S		M	A	D	I	S	O	N
I	N	G	E		C	A	R	A	T		O	T	T	O
S	C	A	R		T	R	A	D	E		N	O	R	M
K	E	N	T		S	A	G	E	S		S	N	E	E

PAGE 76

Sudoku

5	9	2	4	6	8	7	3	1
8	7	1	9	5	3	6	4	2
3	4	6	7	1	2	9	8	5
6	1	7	2	3	9	4	5	8
2	8	4	5	7	1	3	9	6
9	5	3	8	4	6	1	2	7
1	6	9	3	2	5	8	7	4
7	2	8	6	9	4	5	1	3
4	3	5	1	8	7	2	6	9

FRIENDS

Each can have the prefix DIA- to form a new word.

PAGE 77

BrainSnack®—Multiplier

65. Every multiplication is increased by a factor of 1. 13 x (4 + 1) = 65.

SANDWICH

PRINT

PAGE 78

2011 Hit Songs

S	O	L	D		M	A	G	I	C		A	H	S	O
N	I	L	E		I	R	A	N	I		S	O	A	R
E	L	A	L		D	O	Z	E	N		S	W	I	G
R	E	M	I	N	D	M	E		N	E	A	T	L	Y
D	R	A	C	U	L	A		M	A	R	I	O		
			A	N	E		T	I	M	A	L	L	E	N
O	A	S	T	S		P	I	N	O	T		O	V	A
C	L	U	E		W	I	D	E	N		I	V	E	S
H	O	R		P	A	P	E	R		K	N	E	L	T
O	P	E	R	A	T	E	S		C	I	V			
		T	E	N	E	T		A	L	L	E	G	E	D
M	A	H	L	E	R		I	W	A	N	N	A	G	O
A	S	I	A		S	E	G	A	R		T	U	R	N
L	I	N	T		K	I	O	S	K		O	G	E	E
I	N	G	E		I	N	T	H	E		R	E	T	E

PAGE 79
Spot the Differences

LETTERBLOCKS
BLUNDER
BLOOPER

PAGE 80
Binairo

O	I	O	I	O	I	O	I	O	I	I
I	O	I	O	I	O	I	O	I	I	O
I	I	O	O	I	I	O	I	O	O	I
O	O	I	I	O	I	I	O	I	O	I
I	I	O	I	I	O	I	O	O	I	O
O	O	I	O	I	I	O	I	I	O	I
I	I	O	I	O	O	I	O	I	I	O
I	O	I	O	I	I	O	I	O	O	I
O	I	O	I	O	I	I	O	I	I	O
O	I	I	O	I	O	O	I	I	O	I
I	O	I	I	O	O	I	I	O	I	O

DOUBLETALK
SUBJECT

PAGE 81
Cage the Animals

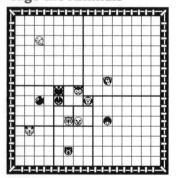

REPOSITION PREPOSITION
ON BEHALF OF

PAGE 82
Themeless

A	B	I	T		S	A	C	H	A		P	E	A	L
S	E	R	E		E	M	A	I	L		U	G	L	I
A	G	O	N		V	I	N	G	T		L	O	S	E
H	U	N	T	E	R	S	T	H	O	M	P	S	O	N
I	N	S	O	L	E	S		C	H	A	I			
			O	K	S		S	H	O	R	T	I	S	H
B	E	R	N	E		T	E	A	R	S		M	O	E
A	R	O	E		D	I	G	I	N		S	I	M	I
T	I	M		S	A	N	E	R		M	E	T	E	R
S	K	E	L	E	T	A	L		L	O	A			
			A	R	A	B		M	I	S	S	I	L	E
H	E	A	R	T	B	R	E	A	K	H	O	T	E	L
A	C	H	Y		A	O	R	T	A		N	A	V	I
T	H	O	N		S	W	I	S	S		A	L	E	S
S	T	Y	X		E	N	N	U	I		L	O	R	E

PAGE 83
Invest

When saving and investing, we put out money for a fee, thereby running a risk.

TRANSADDITION
Add A and find ANAGRAMS
NEVER LIE

PAGE 84
Sunny Weather

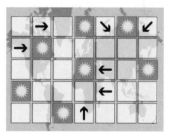

BLOCK ANAGRAM
SLEEPING ROOM

PAGE 85
State Birds

T	F	A	L		L	I	E	D		S	C	R	A	M
A	E	R	O		E	N	V	Y		T	O	O	N	E
C	H	I	C	K	A	D	E	E		E	R	A	T	O
O	R	L	A	N	D	O		S	L	E	N	D	E	R
			T	E	E			A	P	E	R			
A	A	M	I	L	N	E		C	U	L	T	U	R	E
I	S	E	N	T		T	R	A	D	E		N	O	D
S	T	A	G		S	H	A	P	E		S	N	U	G
L	E	D		P	H	A	S	E		S	C	E	N	E
E	R	O	S	I	O	N			R	E	C	O	R	D	S
			W	H	O	A		L	A	R				
A	T	L	A	N	T	A		S	U	R	P	A	S	S
U	K	A	S	E		G	O	L	D	F	I	N	C	H
T	O	R	T	E		E	L	I	E		O	T	O	E
O	S	K	A	R		D	A	D	S		N	I	P	S

PAGE 86
BrainSnack®—Write Me

C. Starting with the middle letter M, to the right and left all letters are always 1, 2, 3 and 4 places further in the alphabet.

END GAME

M I S S P E N D
F I E N D I S H
L E N D A B L E
E N D O C Y S T

PAGE 87
Kakuro

2	9	3		9	7	2		4
7		1	6	5	9		1	5
	9	6	8		4	8	2	6
7	2	8			1	3		9
1		2	1	5		1	5	7
6	2		9	7	1		3	
	7	6			9		1	9
7	6	2	8	4		1	4	
5	8		9	1		2	7	1

MISSING LETTER PROVERB
Barking dogs seldom bite.

PAGE 88

Say Cheese!

F	R	E	T		A	S	K	E	W		A	L	F	A
E	A	S	E		S	T	E	N	O		S	I	O	N
M	O	T	E		H	E	R	O	N		S	M	U	T
M	U	E	N	S	T	E	R		D	O	U	B	L	E
E	L	E	A	N	O	R		N	E	H	R	U		
			G	E	N		F	O	R	M	E	R	L	Y
T	E	P	E	E		P	A	L	E	S		G	E	O
H	E	R	R		D	A	V	I	D		B	E	A	R
A	R	O		S	E	T	O	N		H	O	R	D	E
N	O	V	E	M	B	E	R		P	A	T			
			O	D	E	O	N		P	E	R	H	A	P	S
G	O	L	D	E	N		P	A	R	M	E	S	A	N
A	M	O	I		A	M	A	T	I		R	I	G	A
L	O	N	E		I	M	P	E	L		E	D	E	R
T	O	E	D		R	E	A	R	S		D	E	S	K

PAGE 89

Word Sudoku

T	U	W	E	R	S	B	Y	A
Y	R	S	B	A	W	E	U	T
A	B	E	T	U	Y	W	S	R
E	S	Y	A	B	R	T	W	U
U	A	T	W	S	E	Y	R	B
B	W	R	Y	T	U	S	A	E
S	E	A	U	Y	T	R	B	W
R	T	U	S	W	B	A	E	Y
W	Y	B	R	E	A	U	T	S

LETTERBLOCKS

DESPAIR
HOPEFUL

PAGE 90

Keep Going

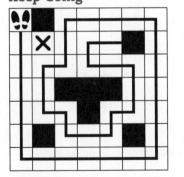

DELETE ONE

Delete A and find SOMERSAULT

PAGE 91

U.S. Cities

A	I	R	S		M	O	S	H	E		R	E	S	T
D	R	E	W		A	B	E	A	M		A	C	T	A
O	M	N	I		G	O	R	K	I		B	R	A	N
S	A	I	N	T	P	E	T	E	R	S	B	U	R	G
			D	W	I			A	P	I				
R	E	P	L	I	E	D		S	T	A	T	E	L	Y
O	T	H	E	R		E	S	M	E		C	I	I	
C	H	A	R	L	O	T	T	E	S	V	I	L	L	E
K	I	S		P	E	E	L		I	M	A	L	L	
S	C	E	P	T	E	R		L	O	C	A	T	E	D
			H	O	R		S	A	G					
C	O	L	O	R	A	D	O	S	P	R	I	N	G	S
O	D	O	N		T	O	P	E	R		N	E	N	E
P	I	L	E		O	V	A	T	E		E	R	A	T
T	E	A	S		R	E	L	A	Y		D	O	T	S

PAGE 92

Sport Maze

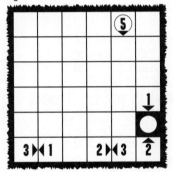

LETTER LINE

ESTABLISH; STABLE, BASIL,
SALT, SLAB

PAGE 93

Sudoku

8	2	4	3	7	5	1	6	9
3	9	1	6	4	2	7	8	5
7	6	5	9	8	1	3	4	2
1	3	2	4	5	8	9	7	6
4	7	6	2	9	3	5	1	8
5	8	9	7	1	6	4	2	3
2	5	3	1	6	4	8	9	7
6	1	7	8	3	9	2	5	4
9	4	8	5	2	7	6	3	1

CHANGELINGS

CONFESSION
INDICTMENT
SETTLEMENT

PAGE 94

BrainSnack®—Kisses

L. Every name has four letters.
The difference of the location
of the letters in the alphabet
always equals 11, 7 and 3.
L - 11 = A + 7 = H - 3 = E.

ONE LETTER LESS OR MORE

RENEGADES

PAGE 95

Leading Men

S	L	A	M		O	H	A	R	A		K	E	N	T
T	O	L	E		S	A	B	E	R		I	S	E	E
I	C	E	T		T	R	E	A	T		E	A	T	S
R	I	C	H	A	R	D	D	R	E	Y	F	U	S	S
			O	B	I			M	A	E				
V	I	A	D	U	C	T		S	U	N	R	I	S	E
I	B	N		T	H	E	M	A	S	K		R	O	D
O	S	E		N	A	G				A	L	E		
L	E	N		H	O	T	T	E	S	T		T	A	N
A	N	T	L	E	R	S		S	C	O	R	E	R	S
			E	R	I		O	L	E					
J	A	M	E	S	G	A	N	D	O	L	F	I	N	I
U	S	E	R		I	D	I	O	T		E	L	A	M
G	A	T	E		N	A	C	R	E		R	I	P	A
S	P	E	D		S	H	E	E	R		S	E	A	N

PAGE 96

Biology

B	S	I	O	E	S	U	G	N	U	F	L	S	O	G
Y	C	I	S	R	A	N	K	E	X	A	G	C	T	S
C	I	A	F	O	I	E	I	N	C	N	E	T	H	A
T	T	I	O	V	C	S	N	S	I	S	O	M	S	O
S	E	R	S	I	E	T	S	R	Y	L	I	M	A	F
D	N	E	S	N	L	U	H	Y	M	O	T	A	N	A
O	E	T	I	M	L	T	I	L	U	N	G	S	I	D
P	G	C	L	O	W	I	P	E	S	L	I	V	T	I
O	E	A	N	O	A	E	S	U	A	P	O	N	E	M
R	R	B	R	G	L	C	R	B	E	A	T	U	R	R
H	O	G	E	S	L	F	E	N	D	I	O	X	I	N
T	V	O	R	M	L	O	E	R	E	F	L	E	X	E
R	I	S	O	A	M	L	N	O	I	T	A	T	U	M
A	N	I	M	O	L	S	P	E	C	I	E	S	F	L
I	R	M	F	O	O	R	G	A	N	I	S	M	E	A
T	A	D	P	O	L	E	N	D	S	I	G	N	S	
M	C	O	F	L	E	C	N	A	T	S	I	S	E	R
I	F	T	A	T	I	B	A	H	E	C	Y	C	L	E

Biology is an exact science
that studies living creatures,
forms of life and signs of life.

UNCANNY TURN

DANCING PARTNER

PAGE 97

BrainSnack®—Odd Number

9. All other numbers are composed of a number of blocks equal to the value of the number.

DOODLE PUZZLE

FatSDomino

PAGE 98

This and That

C	P	A	S		A	M	A	T	I		P	A	L	E
H	E	R	E		S	O	L	O	N		I	B	A	R
E	R	I	E		T	O	A	D	S		G	A	I	T
R	U	S	S	I	A	N	R	O	U	L	E	T	T	E
	T	A	T	I				L	O	O				
F	L	O	W	E	R	S		L	A	U	N	D	E	R
R	E	C		R	E	P	A	I	R	S		O	R	E
E	A	R			L	I	L			N	I	M		
E	V	A		S	P	I	N	A	C	H		R	N	A
R	E	T	R	E	A	T		C	H	E	M	I	S	T
			E	R	R			E	R	I	C			
T	I	G	H	T	R	O	P	E	W	A	L	K	E	R
O	L	E	A		O	R	I	B	I		I	L	I	A
L	E	T	S		T	E	T	O	N		E	E	N	Y
L	A	S	H		S	L	A	N	G		U	S	E	S

PAGE 99

Cage the Animals

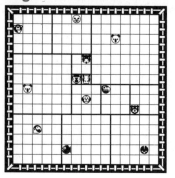

CHANGE ONE

SEA CHANGE

PAGE 100

Binairo

I	I	O	I	O	O	I	I	O	O	I	O
I	I	O	I	O	I	I	O	O	I	O	O
O	O	I	O	I	I	O	O	I	I	O	I
O	I	I	O	I	O	O	I	I	O	I	O
I	O	O	I	O	O	I	I	O	I	I	O
I	O	I	O	I	I	O	O	I	O	O	I
O	I	I	O	O	I	I	O	O	I	O	I
O	I	O	I	I	O	O	I	O	I	I	O
I	O	O	I	O	I	O	O	I	O	I	I
O	O	I	O	I	O	I	I	O	I	O	I
O	I	I	O	O	I	I	O	I	O	I	O
I	O	O	I	I	O	O	I	I	O	O	I

DOODLE PUZZLE

SevenTies

PAGE 101

Tom, Dick and Harry

B	E	E	S		A	C	H	E	S		T	R	A	P
E	T	N	A		P	A	U	L	A		R	U	S	E
S	T	O	P	P	A	R	D	O	R	H	A	N	K	S
S	U	S	P	E	C	T		N	A	I	V	E	S	T
			H	E	H			S	D	I				
M	A	R	I	N	E	S		G	O	D	S	E	N	D
A	M	O	R			W	H	I	T	E		L	I	E
C	A	V	E	T	T	O	R	V	A	N	D	Y	K	E
A	T	E		A	R	O	S	E		A	S	O	R	
W	I	R	E	T	A	P		S	T	A	M	E	N	S
			M	T	V			O	L	E				
O	R	I	O	L	E	S		C	R	O	E	S	U	S
P	O	T	T	E	R	O	R	H	O	U	D	I	N	I
A	L	E	E		S	I	N	A	I		N	O	I	R
H	E	A	R		E	L	A	N	D		A	N	T	S

PAGE 102

Keep Going

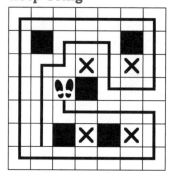

FRIENDS

Each can have the suffix -SHIP to form a new word.

PAGE 103

Word Sudoku

S	A	Z	B	L	G	E	K	Q
B	L	K	Q	E	S	A	G	Z
G	Q	E	Z	K	A	L	B	S
Z	G	B	A	Q	K	S	L	E
A	E	S	G	Z	L	K	Q	B
Q	K	L	S	B	E	G	Z	A
E	Z	G	K	A	Q	B	S	L
L	S	Q	E	G	B	Z	A	K
K	B	A	L	S	Z	Q	E	G

SANDWICH

PAPER

PAGE 104

Cinema Classics

C	A	R	A		C	R	U	E	L		A	M	O	R
L	I	O	N		H	E	A	R	A		M	A	U	I
E	S	S	E		A	D	L	I	B		A	L	T	O
F	L	A	C	C	I	D		C	O	O	N	C	A	T
T	E	N	D	O	N				R	A	D	O	N	
		N	O	R	S	E		H	E	R	A	L	D	S
S	P	A	T	E		L	I	A	R	S		M	O	A
I	R	A	E		C	A	L	L	S		E	M	U	S
T	A	R		T	O	T	A	L		P	A	C	T	S
A	C	Q	U	I	R	E		S	H	A	R	D		
	T	U	N	E	R				A	R	N	O	L	D
N	I	E	L	S	E	N		A	N	T	I	W	A	R
O	C	T	O		C	A	B	I	N		N	E	N	E
D	A	T	A		T	I	A	R	A		G	L	A	D
S	L	E	D		S	L	A	S	H		S	L	I	D

PAGE 105

Sport Maze

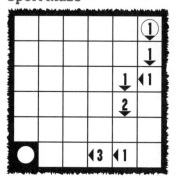

LETTERBLOCKS

AEROBIC
FITNESS

PAGE 106

Sudoku X

9	5	4	8	7	6	2	3	1
3	1	8	2	5	9	6	4	7
2	6	7	4	1	3	8	5	9
7	4	9	6	2	5	3	1	8
5	8	6	9	3	1	4	7	2
1	2	3	7	4	8	9	6	5
4	3	2	1	9	7	5	8	6
8	9	1	5	6	4	7	2	3
6	7	5	3	8	2	1	9	4

REPOSITION PREPOSITION
IN POINT OF

PAGE 107

Wet Set

P	S	S	T		R	A	K	E	D		S	W	A	T
O	P	A	H		E	M	I	L	E		C	A	P	O
W	A	T	E	R	W	O	R	K	S		O	T	T	O
S	T	E	R	E	O	S		S	O	F	T	E	S	T
			M	A	R				L	A	I	R		
T	O	W	A	R	D	S		C	A	N	A	S	T	A
O	P	A	L	S		H	E	A	T	S		D	E	B
N	E	T	S		F	O	S	S	E		M	O	A	N
I	R	E		B	O	A	S	T		D	O	W	S	E
C	A	R	R	O	L	L		S	C	A	N	N	E	R
	C	E	L	L				O	T	T				
B	I	R	D	D	O	G		M	A	U	R	I	C	E
O	D	E	S		W	A	T	E	R	M	E	L	O	N
R	O	S	E		E	T	O	N	S		A	I	N	T
E	L	S	A		R	O	G	U	E		L	E	S	E

PAGE 108

BrainSnack®—Star Tripper

3124. The probe always flies to the next star system with one more yellow star.

DOUBLETALK
WIND

PAGE 109

Word Pyramid

M, (1) me, (2) emu, (3) mule, (4) plume, (5) lumper, (6) crumple, (7) plectrum

TRANSADDITION
Add S and find CANNED MUSIC

PAGE 110

Sunny Weather

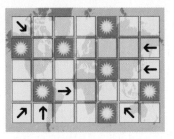

BLOCK ANAGRAM
STEWARDESS

PAGE 111

Case Crackers

E	C	H	O		L	I	L	L	I		S	N	O	W
D	R	I	P		O	N	E	I	L		L	A	M	A
G	I	D	E	O	N	F	E	L	L		E	N	O	S
A	M	E	R	I	G	O		T	I	M	E	C	O	P
R	E	S	A	L	E			N	A	V	Y			
			T	E	R	N		B	O	R	E	D	O	M
A	B	L	E	R		E	L	L	I	S		R	U	E
L	E	A	S		C	I	T	E	S		V	E	S	T
E	A	U		H	O	L	D	S		N	E	W	T	S
C	U	R	E	A	L	L		S	C	A	N			
	A	R	I	L				R	H	E	T	O	R
B	A	H	A	M	A	S		T	A	U	R	I	N	E
E	R	O	S		P	E	R	R	Y	M	A	S	O	N
N	I	L	E		S	A	N	Y	O		T	H	U	D
S	E	T	S		E	T	H	A	N		E	A	R	S

PAGE 112

Sudoku Twin

MISSING LETTER PROVERB
Familiarity breeds contempt.

PAGE 113

Cage the Animals

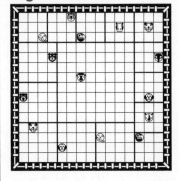

END GAME
H A C I E N D A
A D D E N D U M
R E V E R E N D
D E P E N D E D

PAGE 114

Themeless

C	A	B	A	L		S	A	T	S		A	S	T	A
A	L	A	M	O		I	R	A	N		I	N	O	N
T	E	R	M	S		E	N	J	O	Y	M	E	N	T
S	A	B	O	T	A	G	E		W	O	L	V	E	S
		A	N	I	L	E		B	I	G	E	A	S	Y
M	A	R	I	N	E		T	I	N	A	S			
A	R	I	A		C	L	I	N	G		S	M	U	G
S	E	A			E	G	G					I	L	A
T	A	N	S		T	A	H	O	E		S	N	A	G
			O	P	A	R	T		N	A	T	U	R	E
S	E	L	L	E	R	S		A	D	M	I	T		
P	R	I	V	E	T		O	B	S	O	L	E	T	E
L	I	T	E	R	A	L	L	Y			E	L	M	E	R
I	C	E	R		N	I	L	S		B	E	A	R	S
T	A	R	S		S	P	A	S		A	R	N	I	E

PAGE 115

BrainSnack®—Fingerprints

Piece 2 is the only piece that fits.

DOODLE PUZZLE
One after the Other

PAGE 116

The Spy Who Came in From the Cold

13, 16, 24, 17, 19, 15, 7, 3, 29, 8, 23, 20, 14, 30, 28, 12, 21, 9, 26, 11, 5, 18, 25, 22, 6 =

INV ASI ONB EGI NSA TMI DNI GHT ONT HEF IRS TMO NDA YIN JUN EAT DAW NCO DEN AME OPE RAT ION WAT ERF ALL

INVASION BEGINS AT MID-NIGHT ON THE FIRST MONDAY IN JUNE AT DAWN CODENAME OPERATION WATERFALL

LETTER LINE
REVELATION; RELATIVE, ELEVATOR, RIOT, RETAIN

PAGE 117

On the Beach

A	P	B		P	U	C	E			C	L	A	M
M	O	A		O	S	H	E	A		S	A	O	N	E
I	L	K		S	H	E	L	L	I	N	G	O	U	T
S	K	E	E	T	E	R		I	M	A	Y			
H	A	R	P	E	R		D	E	P	P		U	S	K
	S	I	R		P	I	N	E	A	P	P	L	E	
K	I	D		S	A	R	G		A	T	T	A	I	N
E	N	O	S		L	O	G	I	C		A	N	D	Y
O	F	Z	E	A	L		E	C	H	O		D	E	A
G	R	E	A	T	F	I	R	E		N	S	A		
H	A	N		O	R	B	S		D	E	G	R	E	E
		I	D	E	A		T	R	I	T	O	N	S	
C	H	O	W	D	E	R	H	E	A	D		U	L	T
E	U	R	O	S		S	E	L	M	A		N	A	E
L	E	O	N			P	E	A	S		D	I	S	

PAGE 118

Keep Going

DELETE ONE
Delete S and find
COMPENSATION

PAGE 119

Health

H E A L T H I S S A S T A T E
S U R G E R Y U E C H W O M B
A R O T C O D Y L N M A F R A
D E M E N T I A G F A T C T E
I C O R I Y Z E N Y I S D B Y
A Z U T C C O M R M I P L C
R E A S E N T T H E E G E H S
H A K T I N A N H R U L Y P L
E S E N G C F C A E O A Y S
A L R E M E H E E R U R N T A
T E U D A R E C A L A U A D E
H N D S S P A T A Q S E O O M
P N E U M O N I A N P N X O C
C H R O M O S O M E I N Y L A
L I V A C C I N E W R T G B E
V L P R O S T H E S I S E F A
E N I L A N E R D A N R N R E

Health is a state characterized by complete physical, mental and social welfare.

ONE LETTER LESS OR MORE
ARMCHAIRS

PAGE 120

Expos I

H	O	L	T		S	I	G	M	A		I	S	I	S
A	M	U	R		A	L	I	B	I		N	A	R	A
R	A	R	A		C	I	G	A	R		T	R	E	T
S	H	A	N	G	H	A	I		P	L	E	A	S	E
H	A	Y	S	E	E	D		C	L	U	N	G		
			M	R	T		K	H	A	R	T	O	U	M
H	O	K	I	E		D	U	A	N	E		S	S	A
I	S	N	T		B	E	L	I	E		T	S	A	R
N	E	O		E	L	F	I	N		D	R	A	F	T
T	E	X	T	B	O	O	K		P	O	E			
		V	E	R	S	E		G	R	A	M	M	E	R
R	H	I	N	O	S		B	R	I	S	B	A	N	E
I	O	L	E		O	C	E	A	N		L	O	O	P
M	O	L	T		M	E	A	N	T		E	R	L	E
A	P	E	S		S	O	R	T	S		D	I	A	L

PAGE 121

Sport Maze

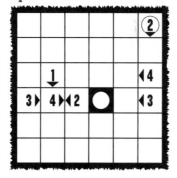

UNCANNY TURN
PUNISHMENT

PAGE 122

Expos II

D	E	E	M		S	C	A	R	P		E	B	R	O
R	U	D	I		H	A	G	A	R		N	A	I	L
A	R	E	S		I	R	A	T	E		O	R	L	E
M	O	N	T	R	E	A	L		S	A	U	C	E	S
A	S	S	A	U	L	T		B	U	L	G	E		
			K	I	D		P	A	M	P	H	L	E	T
M	A	V	E	N		C	A	R	E	S		O	L	A
I	M	A	S		D	A	R	E	S		K	N	O	T
L	M	N		F	E	T	I	D		D	I	A	N	A
S	O	C	R	A	T	E	S		H	O	N			
	O	A	T	H	S		B	A	G	G	A	G	E	
S	A	U	C	E	R		B	R	U	S	S	E	L	S
L	E	V	I		O	N	E	I	L		T	R	O	T
A	R	E	A		N	I	E	C	E		O	I	S	E
G	I	R	L		E	A	S	E	D		N	E	S	S

PAGE 123

Spot the Differences

CHANGE ONE
SHOUTING MATCH

PAGE 124

Sudoku

6	3	5	4	2	8	1	9	7
4	9	7	5	6	1	8	2	3
1	8	2	7	3	9	5	6	4
5	1	4	8	9	2	3	7	6
3	2	8	6	7	4	9	1	5
9	7	6	1	5	3	2	4	8
2	5	1	3	4	7	6	8	9
7	6	9	2	8	5	4	3	1
8	4	3	9	1	6	7	5	2

SQUIRCLES

P A A B H A F O
R N C A U R A X
E G R T B M L A
F O O T B A L L
A L S L U D A Y
B A S E B A L L

PAGE 125

Word Sudoku

S	A	M	X	P	N	R	O	T
N	P	R	O	A	T	X	S	M
X	T	O	S	R	M	P	N	A
M	O	N	R	X	A	T	P	S
A	S	P	M	T	O	N	R	X
R	X	T	P	N	S	A	M	O
O	N	X	A	S	P	M	T	R
T	R	S	N	M	X	O	A	P
P	M	A	T	O	R	S	X	N

DOODLE PUZZLE

MidAfterNoon

PAGE 126

BrainSnack®—Cubism

Group 2. In all the other groups two identically colored cubes are located diagonally across from each other in the corners.

UNCANNY TURN

INDIRA GANDHI

PAGE 127

College Teams I

PAGE 128

Cage the Animals

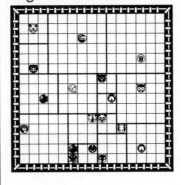

FRIENDS

Each can have the suffix -DOM to form a new word.

PAGE 129

Binairo

1	1	0	1	0	0	1	0	1	1	0
0	1	1	0	1	0	1	1	0	0	1
0	0	1	1	0	1	0	1	1	0	1
1	1	0	1	1	0	1	0	0	1	0
1	0	1	0	0	1	1	0	1	0	1
0	0	1	0	1	1	0	1	1	0	1
0	1	0	1	1	0	1	1	0	1	0
1	0	1	0	1	0	0	1	1	0	0
1	1	0	0	1	1	0	1	0	0	1
0	1	1	0	1	0	1	0	1	1	0
1	0	0	1	0	1	0	1	0	1	1

SANDWICH

NAIL

PAGE 130

College Teams II

S	C	A	R		A	D	I	E	U		S	N	A	P
P	O	L	A		B	A	C	O	N		P	O	L	E
A	N	T	I		S	I	E	N	A		A	T	E	E
S	T	A	N	F	O	R	D		F	E	R	R	E	R
M	E	R	C	U	R	Y		C	R	E	T	E		
			O	R	B		C	H	A	R	A	D	E	S
N	E	P	A	L		P	O	L	I	O		A	L	I
I	C	E	T		F	L	O	O	D		O	M	A	N
P	R	N		O	R	A	L	E		M	I	E	N	S
S	U	N	S	P	O	T	S		B	E	N			
		S	E	E	N	O		C	O	N	T	O	U	R
N	A	T	A	N	T		C	O	L	U	M	B	I	A
I	W	A	S		I	R	E	N	E		E	E	N	Y
L	E	T	O		E	E	L	E	R		N	A	T	O
E	D	E	N		R	A	T	S	O		T	H	A	N

PAGE 131

Astronomy

Astronomy is one of the few sciences in which amateurs can play an active role.

LETTERBLOCKS

ENGLAND
GERMANY

PAGE 132

Keep Going

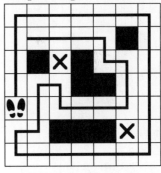

REPOSITION PREPOSITION

NOTWITHSTANDING

PAGE 133

Themeless

M	A	R	I	S		S	P	A	T		D	I	S	S
A	L	O	N	E		T	A	C	H		E	T	C	H
R	A	T	H	E		I	N	T	E	R	F	E	R	E
V	I	T	A	M	I	N	S		R	O	A	M	E	D
		E	L	E	C	T		R	E	B	U	S	E	S
L	A	R	E	D	O		E	A	S	E	L			
E	N	D	S		N	U	B	I	A		T	A	C	O
A	D	A			L	B	S				T	O	D	
H	Y	M	N		K	N	E	E	D		H	A	L	E
		I	L	I	A	D		A	M	E	N	D	S	
O	B	S	C	E	N	E		D	I	A	R	Y		
N	A	T	H	A	N		H	I	S	T	O	R	I	C
E	R	R	O	N	E	O	U	S		T	I	A	R	A
A	R	I	L		A	V	E	C		E	N	T	E	R
L	E	A	S		R	O	Y	S		R	E	E	D	S

PAGE 134

Sport Maze

DOUBLETALK
STICK

PAGE 135

Kakuro

6	1	7		1	5		3	2
9	2		2	9	3		4	1
5	3	7	6		8	1		3
8		8				3	5	6
	9	4	8		6	7	4	
1	5		1	7	3		1	2
3	2	7		2	1	8		4
8		4		6		6	7	8
4	2	9	7		1	7	8	9

TRANSADDITION
Add S and find CREDENTIALS

PAGE 136

Themeless

S	P	A	S	M		B	O	S	C		S	L	A	B
H	A	S	T	A		O	R	R	A		T	O	D	O
A	N	T	O	N	I	O	B	A	N	D	E	R	A	S
H	E	R	O	I	N	E	S		N	O	R	R	I	S
		O	G	L	E	D		C	O	N	N	E	R	Y
E	N	D	E	A	R		B	A	N	T	U			
L	E	O	S		T	S	A	R	S		M	A	Y	O
L	E	M			T	R	E			R	E	B		
I	D	E	M		D	A	R	Y	L		O	S	L	O
		A	E	R	I	E		E	U	R	O	P	E	
S	P	E	C	T	E	R		S	A	T	I	N		
E	R	R	A	N	D		O	P	P	O	S	I	T	E
G	A	R	B	A	G	E	D	I	S	P	O	S	A	L
E	D	E	R		E	V	E	L		I	N	T	R	A
R	O	D	E		S	E	A	L		A	S	S	E	T

PAGE 137

BrainSnack®—Painter

Paint 3. 6/8 of a square was colored in with paints 1 and 4, 5/8 of a square for paint 2 and 7/8 for paint 3.

BLOCK ANAGRAM
SPINAL CORD

PAGE 138

Word Sudoku

R	A	B	I	T	V	L	D	E
D	E	V	L	A	R	T	B	I
I	L	T	B	E	D	R	A	V
A	V	I	R	D	L	E	T	B
B	R	E	T	I	A	D	V	L
T	D	L	V	B	E	A	I	R
E	I	D	A	R	B	V	L	T
V	B	R	D	L	T	I	E	A
L	T	A	E	V	I	B	R	D

MISSING LETTER PROVERB
Silence is golden.

PAGE 139

BrainSnack®—Number Block

7. Every number equals the sum of the number of blocks to the right of the number and the number of blocks under the number.

END GAME

A S C E N D E R
U N B E N D E D
R E M E N D E D
A M E N D F U L

PAGE 140

Doctor Who

A	M	O	S		T	R	O	I	K	A		B	E	D
S	O	R	A		H	A	S	S	A	N		U	N	A
S	T	E	L	S	E	W	H	E	R	E		R	O	Y
T	O	O	T	O	O		A	A	A		A	N	K	A
			I	A	M	S		S	T	A	R	S	I	N
F	R	A	N	K	E	N	S	T	E	I	N			
A	I	D	E		G	O	O			N	E	G	E	V
I	N	A		L	A	B	C	O	A	T		U	R	I
R	O	M	E	O			K	A	N		P	R	O	S
			G	R	E	G	O	R	Y	H	O	U	S	E
R	O	M	A	I	N	E		S	O	A	P			
A	B	C	D		S	A	W		T	R	O	J	A	N
P	E	C		Y	U	R	I	Z	H	I	V	A	G	O
I	S	O		B	R	U	L	E	E		E	V	E	R
D	E	Y		K	E	P	L	E	R		R	A	R	A

PAGE 141

Sudoku X

1	7	3	9	8	5	6	4	2
2	4	5	3	6	1	8	9	7
6	9	8	4	2	7	5	3	1
7	2	9	6	1	3	4	5	8
5	8	6	2	7	4	9	1	3
3	1	4	8	5	9	2	7	6
8	5	1	7	4	2	3	6	9
9	6	7	5	3	8	1	2	4
4	3	2	1	9	6	7	8	5

UNCANNY TURN
DRUMSTICKS

PAGE 142

Cage the Animals

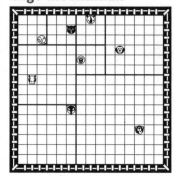

CHANGELINGS

L O C O M O T I V E
M E C H A N I C A L
H O R S E P O W E R

PAGE 143

Homophones

C	H	A	R		E	M	B	E	D		C	P	A	S
A	I	D	E		L	E	E	Z	A		O	R	L	O
S	T	A	T	I	O	N	A	R	Y		M	I	E	N
T	U	N	I	S	I	A		A	B	S	E	N	C	E
S	P	O	R	T	S		R	O	T	C				
			E	L	E	E		P	E	N	S	I	V	E
T	E	P	E	E		A	R	E	A	S		P	A	L
O	U	R	S		W	R	E	C	K		D	L	I	I
M	R	I		W	A	L	D	O		S	A	E	N	S
B	O	N	M	O	T	S		S	E	E	M			
		C	O	V	E			N	E	P	A	L	I	
S	P	I	D	E	R	S		A	L	T	E	R	E	D
N	O	P	E		S	T	A	T	I	O	N	E	R	Y
U	N	A	S		K	I	T	E	S		E	C	O	L
G	E	L	T		I	R	A	N	T		D	A	I	S

PAGE 144

Keep Going

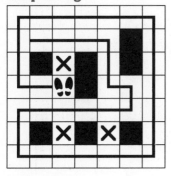

DELETE ONE
Delete S and find FANATICISM

PAGE 145

Telecommunications

In the past, if you wanted to phone someone then you pressed a button to attract the attention of the switchboard operator.

CHANGE ONE
COLD SWEAT

PAGE 146

First Name Last

E	G	G	S		C	O	H	O		A	S	H	E	R
M	O	R	E		A	R	I	A		S	A	U	C	Y
B	L	A	C	K	J	A	C	K		P	I	N	T	A
E	D	I	T	I	O	N		S	K	E	L	T	O	N
D	A	N	I	E	L		E	C	O	L				
		O	L	E	S		E	N	T	R	I	E	S	
S	I	G	N		D	W	E	L	T		S	N	A	P
W	A	R		U	R	L			D	R	Y			
I	G	E	T		A	N	G	E	R		L	A	S	S
T	O	E	R	I	N	G		N	E	N	E			
	N	A	N	G			B	A	A	B	A	A		
V	I	S	I	T	E	D		P	E	R	S	O	N	S
I	R	E	N	E		R	O	C	K	C	H	R	I	S
L	A	T	E	R		A	B	B	A		E	N	S	E
A	S	H	E	N		G	I	S	H		D	E	E	T

PAGE 147

BrainSnack®—Energy Saver

9. The rooms located one floor higher use the average of the two rooms below.

LETTER LINE
FORMIDABLE; BAILED, LIMBO, BRIEF, BLADE, BEDLAM

PAGE 148

Monkey Business

The Lion the Witch and the Wardrobe
The Cat in the Hat
The Ugly Duckling
Charlotte's Web
The Twits

ONE LETTER LESS OR MORE
COALITION

PAGE 149

Last Name First

H	A	R	D		S	T	A	R	R		A	W	L	S
O	B	O	E		T	H	R	E	E		G	H	A	T
L	I	T	T	L	E	R	I	C	H		A	I	D	E
D	E	C	E	I	V	E	D		E	A	S	T	E	R
			S	K	E	W		M	A	N	S	E		
C	A	C	T	U	S		C	A	R	N	I	V	A	L
A	C	H	E	D		W	O	R	S	E		A	D	E
R	O	A	D		S	I	N	G	E		F	N	M	A
O	D	S		R	E	N	E	E		C	A	N	E	S
M	E	E	T	I	N	G	S		P	L	I	A	N	T
	C	R	O	S	S		H	A	I	R				
T	A	H	I	T	I		R	E	I	M	P	O	S	E
A	L	E	X		B	R	O	W	N	B	L	A	I	R
L	E	V	I		L	U	M	E	T		A	H	A	B
K	A	Y	E		E	G	A	D	S		Y	U	L	E

PAGE 150

Sport Maze

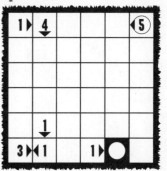
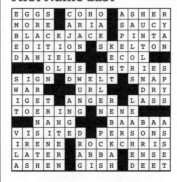

UNCANNY TURN
MOMMY

PAGE 151

Word Sudoku

P	K	Q	G	N	C	A	M	I
I	A	M	P	K	Q	G	C	N
G	N	C	I	M	A	K	Q	P
M	I	A	K	Q	N	P	G	C
C	G	K	M	A	P	N	I	Q
Q	P	N	C	I	G	M	K	A
N	Q	G	A	C	K	I	P	M
A	M	P	Q	G	I	C	N	K
K	C	I	N	P	M	Q	A	G

DOODLE PUZZLE
CoffeeBreak

PAGE 152

Spot the Differences

DELETE ONE
Delete N and find CROUPIERS

PAGE 153

Wines

B	E	E	T		A	M	B	E	R		S	P	O	T
E	R	S	E		R	E	E	S	E		H	I	D	E
A	N	T	A		T	A	R	T	S		E	N	I	D
R	I	E	S	L	I	N	G		O	N	I	O	N	S
D	E	E	P	E	S	T		B	U	I	L	T		
		O	A	T		M	O	N	T	A	N	A	N	
L	U	Z	O	N		F	O	O	D	S		O	N	O
O	L	I	N		C	A	P	E	S		S	I	N	O
C	A	N		A	I	D	E	D		A	K	R	O	N
I	N	F	O	R	M	E	D		C	L	I			
	A	L	I	A	S		R	O	L	L	E	R	S	
T	I	N	D	E	R		S	E	M	I	L	L	O	N
A	N	D	I		R	E	C	A	P		F	A	L	A
T	R	E	E		O	V	A	T	E		U	T	E	P
A	I	L	S		N	A	T	A	L		L	E	S	S

PAGE 154

Sudoku X

5	2	4	7	3	8	1	9	6
9	8	6	4	2	1	3	5	7
7	1	3	5	9	6	4	2	8
6	4	2	9	1	3	8	7	5
8	3	9	6	7	5	2	4	1
1	5	7	8	4	2	9	6	3
3	7	1	2	5	4	6	8	9
4	9	8	3	6	7	5	1	2
2	6	5	1	8	9	7	3	4

FRIENDS

Each can have the suffix -AL to form a new word

PAGE 155

Cage the Animals

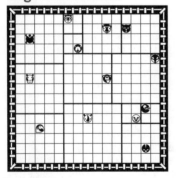

SANDWICH

HEAD

PAGE 156

Seafarers

E	L	B	E			I	O	W	A			B	A	D
N	O	E	L	S		B	R	A	N	T		O	N	E
J	O	E	L	Y	F	I	S	H	E	R		A	T	E
O	F	F	E	R	E	D		S	W	E	A	T	E	R
Y	A	Y		I	L	E	S		N	A	B			
		S	A	L	M	O	N	P	C	H	A	S	E	
T	A	K	E	N		R	O	T	H		S	A	P	
O	L	I	N		G	O	T	T	A		N	I	K	E
M	O	S		C	A	R	E		A	N	N	I	E	
B	U	S	T	E	R	C	R	A	B	B	E			
	I	A	L		S	P	A	R		A	S	S		
B	E	N	N	E	T	T		P	R	A	I	R	I	E
A	R	G		B	O	B	C	L	A	M	P	E	T	T
T	I	E		S	T	A	R	E		S	O	N	I	A
H	E	R		E	R	O	S		D	A	N	E		

PAGE 157

BrainSnack®—Parking Space

Car 11. All white and red cars are parked nose inward. All blue cars are parked with the nose outward except car 11.

LETTERBLOCKS

SPIDER
CRICKET

PAGE 158

Agriculture

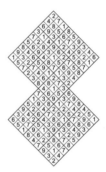

Agriculture produces food as well as other goods such as flowers, fur, leather and biofuel.

CHANGE ONE

HOT CAKES

PAGE 159

Weird Al

H	A	S	H		A	N	I	L	S		C	H	O	U
A	R	C	A		T	O	M	E	I		R	E	N	T
R	E	A	L		A	R	I	A	L		A	X	L	E
P	E	R	F	O	R	M	T	H	I	S	W	A	Y	
O	L	Y	M	P	I	A		C	U	L	M			
		A	E	S		S	C	O	R	S	E	S	E	
P	I	P	S		A	T	O	N	E		T	O	P	
O	D	E	T	O	A	S	U	P	E	R	H	E	R	O
E	E	R		L	I	E	N	S		A	R	T	S	
M	A	I	N	D	R	A	G		A	M	Y			
	S	E	E	S		S	H	A	S	T	A	S		
I	C	A	N	T	W	A	T	C	H	T	H	I	S	
O	D	O	R		R	I	C	O	H		A	R	M	S
R	O	P	E		I	S	T	O	O		C	E	E	S
B	L	E	D		P	H	I	L	O		K	E	D	S

PAGE 160

Sudoku Twin

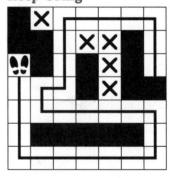

REPOSITION PREPOSITION

ALONGSIDE

PAGE 161

Keep Going

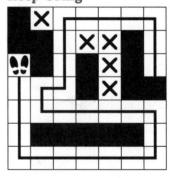

DOUBLETALK

SECOND

PAGE 162

Leading Ladies

PAGE 163

Monkey Business

Goodnight Moon
The Very Hungry Caterpillar
Are You My Mother?
What Do People Do All Day?
Dear Zoo

CHANGE ONE

LIGHT YEAR

PAGE 164

Word Pyramid

T, (1) at, (2) ant, (3) Etna,
(4) agent, (5) eating,
(6) heating, (7) teaching

TRANSADDITION

Add A and find EDUCATION

PAGE 165

Best-Sellers I

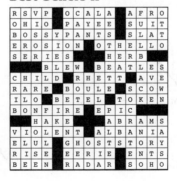

PAGE 166

Sunny Weather

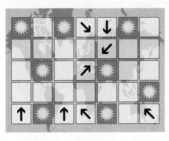

BLOCK ANAGRAM

CRUISE MISSILE

PAGE 167

BrainSnack®—Flag It

Flag M. Every pair includes a red and white flag. The other flag in the pair has the same pattern but all the colors are different. Only one color is different on flag M.

END GAME

F O R E F E N D
E X P E N D E R
L E G E N D R Y
E N D O G E N Y

PAGE 168

Best-Sellers II

PAGE 169

The Puzzled Librarian

1) *Absalom, Absalom!*
2) *The Way of All Flesh*
3) *I Know Why the Caged Bird Sings*
4) *Far From the Madding Crowd*
5) *The Cricket on the Hearth*
6) *Ah, Wilderness!*
7) *Tender Is the Night*
8) *All the King's Men*
9) *The Waste Land*
10) *Of Mice and Men*

MISSING LETTER PROVERB

Fight fire with fire.

PAGE 170

Photography

The word photography is derived from Greek; it literally means writing with light.

DELETE ONE

Delete L and find COUNTERFEITER

PAGE 171

Cage the Animals

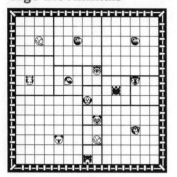

CHANGELINGS

C A N N E L L O N I
V E G E T A B L E S
P A T I S S E R I E

PAGE 172

Number Cluster

2	2	4	4	4	4	
8	8	7	7	7	7	
8	5	5	5	6	7	
8	5	1	5	6	7	
8	8	8	8	6	7	
3	3	3	6	6	6	

LETTER LINE

MOUSETRAPS; MAESTRO,
TAMPER, STREAM, MASTER

PAGE 173

Spot the Differences

DELETE ONE

Delete one S and find
PLATITUDES

PAGE 174

Relaxation

A	C	E	D		M	O	N	O		A	B	O	M	B
L	O	R	I		E	B	A	Y		M	O	V	I	E
T	H	E	S	U	N	I	S	S	H	I	N	I	N	G
O	N	I	O	N		A	T	A		A	D	E	S	
		W	I	S	H		E	V	E	N				
G	E	N	T	L	E	B	R	E	E	Z	E	S		
A	R	T	S		A	R	A			K	A	L	E	L
R	A	H		D	W	A	Y	N	E	S		I	D	A
K	I	N	T	E		O	E	R		D	O	G	S	
	L	O	W	E	R	H	U	M	I	D	I	T	Y	
		I	D	E	A		O	K	R	A				
E	G	A	N		I	R	K		A	M	E	B	A	
B	R	O	K	E	N	L	A	W	N	M	O	W	E	R
B	E	N	I	N		O	T	I	C		N	E	A	L
S	W	E	E	T		W	E	G	O		D	R	N	O

ANSWERS TO QUICK AND DO YOU KNOW

p 15: A pontification
p 17: Charles Darwin
p 19: *Roots*
p 21: Queenstown, Ireland (renamed Cobh in 1922)
p 23: A clutch
p 25: 14—China borders Afghanistan, Bhutan, India, Kazakhstan, Kyrgyzstan, Laos, Mongolia, Myanmar (Burma), Nepal, North Korea, Pakistan, Russia, Tajikistan and Vietnam
p 27: Let the buyer beware
p 29: A jump where the legs criss-cross in the air
p 31: Herbert Hoover
p 33: Trigger
p 35: 1
p 37: Ursula Andress
p 39: 6
p 41: Sean Connery
p 43: The Repeal of Prohibition
p 45: Pessomancy
p 47: September, April, June and November
p 49: St. Matthew
p 51: Full of grace
p 53: A muster
p 55: Cooked crab
p 57: 50 meters
p 59: Ulysses S. Grant
p 61: A fish
p 63: Diamond
p 65: Clowns
p 67: Ten Lords a-leaping
p 69: Bashful, Doc, Dopey, Grumpy, Happy, Sleepy and Sneezy
p 71: DCC

p 73: Switzerland
p 75: Melchior, Caspar and Balthazar
p 77: Straw Weight (limit 105 lbs.)
p 79: Luanda
p 81: Bulgaria
p 83: Varieties or types of tea
p 85: A knot is equal to one nautical mile per hour (1.151 mph/1.852 kph)
p 87: Silver
p 89: A handstamp for commemorative purposes
p 91: Marie Curie
p 93: A position where any move is disadvantageous
p 95: Eros
p 97: Physics
p 99: Chukkers
p 101: Sadness
p 103: Squirrel
p 105: A growler
p 107: Crane
p 109: Rocky Marciano
p 111: Eleanor Rigby
p 113: Sergei Prokofiev
p 115: Spanish
p 117: Colon
p 119: Crossing bridges
p 121: Italian
p 123: "A"
p 125: A jenny
p 127: Hunter S. Thompson
p 129: A lion
p 131: A nye
p 133: 28
p 135: Frisbee
p 137: Space bar
p 139: Smallpox
p 141: Karaoke
p 143: George Washington, Abraham Lincoln, Thomas Jefferson and Theodore Roosevelt
p 145: A heart
p 147: Cameron Diaz
p 149: Anne, Charlotte and Emily
p 151: *A Christmas Carol*
p 153: Penguin
p 155: August 16, 1977
p 157: Right
p 159: DeLorean DMC-12
p 161: Golf
p 163: Huskies
p 165: Batman
p 167: Prunes
p 169: Balaclava
p 171: *Moby Dick*
p 173: Wilma